THE SAMARITANS

to help those tempted to suicide or despair

More than 5,000 people in every year commit suicide in the British Isles.

In response to this problem and from the inspiration of Chad Varah, the Rector of St. Stephen Walbrook, London, in November 1953 there came into being a uniquely personal service, called The Samaritans, to help those tempted to suicide or despair.

Since its quiet beginnings The Samaritans has grown into an international organization with over sixty-five Branches in the United Kingdom alone, many overseas, and similar organizations, inspired by The Samaritans, in other countries.

The book is introduced by Chad Varah, who gives an account of the growth of the organization and all the aims and ideals which inspire it. Doctors, priests and a psychiatric social worker go on to describe some of the problems with which Samaritans have to deal, and outline some of the ways in which they tackle them.

The book will be of great importance to all professionally concerned with the welfare of the lonely and the desperate. But the story of The Samaritans is primarily one about ordinary people. The book should therefore appeal to everyone whose heart is set on man's humanity to man.

A list of the addresses and telephone numbers of all existing Samaritan Branches, and the addresses of affiliated organizations overseas, is included.

Papers by Paul de Berker
Mary Bruce
Richard Fox
Doris Odlum
W. Linford Rees
Eric Reid
Louis Rose
Erwin Stengel
W. Lawton Tonge
Chad Varah
H. J. Walton

The Samaritans

to help those tempted
to suicide or despair

*Edited with an Introduction
by Chad Varah*

Constable London

Published by Constable and Company Ltd
10–12 Orange Street London WC2
© 1965 The Samaritans
First published 1965

Printed in Great Britain by
C. Tinling & Co. Ltd
Liverpool, London and Prescot

CONTENTS

This book is dedicated
to all those tempted
to suicide or despair

No man is an *Iland*, intire of it selfe; every man is a peece of the *Continent*, a part of the *maine*; if a *Clod* bee washed away by the *Sea*, *Europe* is the lesse, as well as if a *Promontorie* were, as well as if a *Mannor* of thy *friends* or of *thine owne* were; any mans *death* diminishes *me*, because I am involved in *Mankinde*; And therefore never send to know for whom the *bell* tolls; It tolls for *thee*.

John Donne, *Devotions*

Introduction

Chad Varah

The Samaritans are several thousand men and women who dedicate a generous part of their leisure time to the prevention of suicide. Theirs are the quiet, unhurried voices which, at any hour of the day or night, any day of the year, answer one of over fifty emergency telephones with the words, "The Samaritans—can I help you?" Because of their devotion to their chosen task, and their loving concern for those who are at the end of their tether and thought nobody cared, several thousand human beings are alive who might otherwise be dead. Thousands more live more happily and hopefully because of the friendship of the Samaritans—some of whom were once themselves in the position of feeling they could not go on but found that a Samaritan emergency telephone was *their* lifeline. In sixty-six centres at home and overseas, Samaritans are turning up regularly on duty, manning the telephones, receiving those who call in person, spending countless hours in patient and usually undramatic befriending of people who often have no one else to turn to, and sometimes, more dramatically, speeding to the scene of someone's last struggle with despair. They do not appear on television, and their names are not reported in the Press; they receive no praise and look for no thanks; and they are blissfully unaware that they are the salt of the earth. They create oases of humanity in the desert of man's selfishness and indifference, and only when their atti-

9

tude is adopted by the greater part of the population will the sickness of our society be healed.

Whenever I hear myself referred to as the Founder of The Samaritans, I want to protest: "I didn't found them—I didn't even *find* most of them. The first of them found *me*, and without them The Samaritans would not exist." I chose the name, not only because the parable of the Good Samaritan inspires our work, but because it implies a collection of *people*, in each of whom the purpose of the fellowship is to be fulfilled, whereas a 'Society for the Prevention of Suicide' would have conjured up the idea of officials and committees and an organization rather than a fellowship of compassionate people any one of whom could be relied upon not to pass by on the other side. A person who is in despair and tempted to take his own life would not risk being told, "I will put your application before our Board, which meets on Wednesday week." He needs a compassionate fellow human being to whom he can say, "Will *you* help me? Now?" Each Samaritan invites this appeal. Naturally, there has to be an organization if a Samaritan is always to be available however many people seek help at once, and if various kinds of professional help are also to be provided; but the organization exists in order to put the right person in the right place at the right time.

It all began with an offer of personal help. When I made it known on November 2nd, 1953, that people contemplating suicide were invited to telephone me at MANsion House 9000, I did not think of myself as founding an organization, still less a world movement,

as it has now become. It was a very small act of obed-
ience on my part and I never dreamt what extensive use
God would be able to make of it. Indeed, I hardly
looked ahead at all: if I had known what I was letting
myself in for in the first few years, I do not know whether
I should have dared to make that rash offer. I have a
tendency to act on impulse, and whilst sometimes I
have had cause to regret this, at other times I have
been glad eventually that I landed myself in a position
that scared me but in which it was easier to go on than
to turn back. I suppose this is a way of trying to overcome an inherent timidity. When I read, in the summer
of 1953, that there were three suicides a day in Greater
London, in spite of our extensive Medical and Social
services, I thought something ought to be done about
it—and if I had had any sense, I would have written to
The Times and said so. Instead, I asked myself whether
I ought not to do something about it. I suppose this
comes partly from having been blessed with parents who
were accustomed to do what they conceived to be their
duty rather than to wonder vaguely why the Govern-
ment did not do something, and partly through being
the eldest of nine children, which leads one to feel
responsible for others and to think one ought to look
after them when necessary. I know one has to be on the
watch against being overprotective or doing things for
people which it would be better if they did themselves,
but one cannot care about people without feeling responsible for them, and one just has to watch it that a
helping hand does not become interference. I am convinced that the best therapy is non-directive, but I shall
not be doctrinaire about it, for I find there are times

when it is kindest to use whatever authority you have, particularly in situations where a person is just incapable of making a decision for himself and when a decision must be made. It is like teaching a child to walk: if you do not let it go for fear it will fall and hurt itself, it will never learn, but if you go to the other extreme, it might fall into the fire. It is not only children who *need* at times to be told what to do, but also adults whom circumstances have brought almost to the helpless dependance of childhood, though of course this dependence must be ended as rapidly as possible. I once had a client from my native Barton-on-Humber who was hesitating to do what seemed to me a plain duty (something I thought in his heart he really wanted to do), so I told him what to do and he obeyed and it worked out happily. He said to me afterwards: "Thoo sounded just like tha faäther, Maäster Chad—us allus did as 'e said." It is true that parishioners were accustomed to go to my father for straightforward advice, and being a man of principle he could usually give it with assurance, and people usually (if not "allus") followed it, with good results. It seems to me that if you have some authority, you are bound to influence those who consult you, whether you use it to direct bewildered or frightened people what step to take next, or whether, as more often happens, you use it 'non-directively', i. e. to direct the person to consider with you what step he wants to take. Mostly it is better to let the other person take as long as he needs to find out what it is that *he* wants to do.

I remember one woman who was so verbose that no one ever listened to her. When she came to see me, she was talking before the door opened, and did not stop for well over an hour. She did not even pause to take a drink of the tea I offered her, lest I should slip a word in edgeways. At first this torrent of words was incoherent and repetitious, but gradually, as I continued to give her my full attention, the nature of her quite complicated situation began to be clarified. She was by no means unintelligent, but like some people doing an addition sum, she could only think if she did it aloud. At long last she paused, and took a drink of her cold tea. All the time she had been talking I had been sorting out her problems, and I was quite pleased with the cleverness of my solution. Now was my big chance, and I took it: I said nothing. She put down her cup, stood up and shook me warmly by the hand, and told me mine was the best advice she had ever had and she would go away and do exactly as I had suggested and was sure it would work out splendidly. Throughout the interview I had not said a word, unless you count "Mmmm". That does not mean I had not said anything: my attention to her conveyed sympathy with her plight and respect for her good intentions. Most people who ask for advice do not want advice, they want approval for what they are going to do anyway; and this I gave her. I do not suppose anyone had ever bothered to hear her out before. I might have felt a pang for my own beautiful solution if I had not still been ashamed of an occasion a few weeks before when I had gone with a chap to a difficult encounter to speak on his behalf, and the other person had not allowed me to speak, so I had to listen whilst the client said badly what I flattered myself I would have said well. We got what we came for, and

I did some soul searching and reminded myself that the object of our journey was this, and not to demonstrate what a good advocate I was. It is a blessing that duties come too thick and fast to allow time for the temptation to pat oneself on the back when one of them has been done successfully—or, for that matter, for profitless repining over failures.

An example of direction succeeding where non-directive methods would not have been quick enough if they had worked at all was in the case of a young woman who was not going to deserve that adjective much longer and whose first, and probably last, chance of marriage had come whilst her widowed mother, with whom she lived, still needed her. The mother was evidently one of those sweet tyrants who are more frustrating than sour ones: a sofa invalid whom I guessed to be as tough as old boots, living on her daughter's vitality and, like a vampire, getting younger as the latter got older. There was no financial or even servant problem, but the mother had convinced her daughter that to leave her in order to get married (which would involve moving some way away) would cause the mother's death. The conflict between her 'duty' to her mother and her desire for a life of her own with the man she loved had led her to a suicidal act which nearly proved fatal, and I was not slow to point out that if she had died, neither of them would have had her. The conflict could be resolved only by her seeing one claim as a duty and the other as an occasion of sin, and I told her firmly that she must let her suitor marry her and take her away, because it was bad for her mother's soul as well as her own that she should remain tied to someone she hated. "But I love Mama!" she protested. "Nonsense," I said. "Nobody could love that selfish old bloodsucker, and I bet your father's death was a blessed release for him. She's conditioned you to believe it's your duty to 'love' her in the sense of pandering to all her whims, but if you didn't think it was wicked to say so you'd admit you hate her." After a while she said quietly, "Yes, I hate her," and I had a glimpse of her private hell from which the only escape was suicide, or murder—unless a man firmly carried her away. For once I became a Bible-thumper. "Therefore," I quoted, "shall a man leave his father and mother, and cleave unto his wife!" "But I'm not a man," she objected unconvincingly. "The point is," I thundered, "does he make you feel a woman?" The way she looked as she answered "Yes" gave me good hope that we had won, and so it proved. A year later the marriage was still happy and the mother still cumbering the earth. I do not think anything could have prised that young woman loose in time except a priest prophesying at her forcefully about God's will. I also gave her a briefing on sex in marriage, so she had a carrot in front as well as a goad behind.

Throughout my ministry, I had always been more interested in counselling than in other parts of parochial work, and I started giving pastoral preparation for marriage, including sexual instruction, to young couples whilst I was still an unmarried Deacon. I was happiest when dealing with people one by one, in a sick-room or hospital, in my study or the Confessional, by a coffin or in a Condemned Cell; and apart from taking services,

I felt I was being a Priest when I was doing this rather than when I was keeping the parochial machinery grinding on. I felt I had not been ordained in order to spend seven-eighths of my time as a bored administrator and unsuccessful commercial traveller, and although I was happy looking after a congregation of a hundred wonderful people in a parish of ten thousand in South London, with the Chaplaincy of a hospital thrown in, the idea of reversing these proportions and being able to spend seven-eighths of my time being a Priest (as I understood this) appeared to me more a yielding to inclination than any sort of sacrifice. I have always believed that vocation is not usually a matter of the Archangel Gabriel yelling clear instructions at one through a celestial megaphone, but more a matter of God working His will by insinuating promptings into our circumstances and interests and inclinations, not because inclinations cannot be temptations, but because we mostly do best what we have some aptitude for and like doing. In other words, God's 'call' is a challenge to us to find out what we are *for*. I did not find out what I was for until I was forty-two.

The idea then of giving all my time to those with whom life has dealt so harshly that they are not sure they want to go on with it, appealed to me. "Three suicides a day in Greater London" did not appear to me to be simply statistics, but desolate people whom I could imagine dying miserably in lonely rooms. That is one of the penalties of being a visualizer—a freakish condition I inherited from my mother. A visualizer has a vivid visual imagination, and sees pictures in his mind's eye in 3D and in colour. It was because of this that I was

Staff Script-writer for *Eagle* and *Girl* for twelve years, and I remember that when I was told one day that each copy of *Eagle* was read by three and a quarter boys, I shuddered at the grisly picture of a bloodstained quarter of a boy holding *Eagle* in his only hand and reading it with half an eye. This faculty makes it very painful reading about atrocities and disasters in newspapers, and I was haunted by the pictures of a different person every eight hours dying by his or her own hand in the city in which I lived.

Because my early training was scientific, a number of pertinent questions posed themselves in my mind. What sort of people were behind these dreadful statistics? Were they all mentally ill? Did they need psychiatry? If so, why did they not apply for it? Or if they did, why did it not save them? Were some of them helpable by professional social workers? If so, why did they not apply to these? Doubtless, great numbers of potential suicides *were* helped by psychiatrists and other doctors, by social workers, and by clergymen and ministers, but there were still three a day in London who died by their own hands. What, if anything, could have saved them? In addition to the suicidal acts which led to death, there were perhaps ten times as many whose act was not fatal. Was it necessary for all of these to endanger their lives or harm themselves in order to draw attention to their plight, or might they be willing to accept help if it were available without recourse to such desperate measures?

There were some clues to the answers to these questions. A great many people have a fear of psychiatry and in particular of mental hospitals, and this fear is often strongest in those who have need of such services. Many people who need psychiatry are brought to it only by the intervention of anxious relatives or friends. What of those who have neither?

Coroners' verdicts nearly always assumed that a person who had committed suicide was mentally ill at the time. Was this assumption justified, or was it a merciful fiction allowing the remains to be buried in consecrated ground, thus avoiding further distress to already grieved relatives? People close to the deceased, often intelligent observers, were sometimes doubtful whether the emotional disturbance which led to the suicidal act was of the nature of a mental illness treatable by psychiatry. (Subsequent research into this question has shown that thirty per cent of those who do commit suicide have had psychiatric treatment, and it is estimated that half as many again ought to have had such treatment. Ignoring the fact that the thirty per cent died in spite of the treatment they had had, this still leaves fifty-five per cent, a majority, of whom it appeared true to say that they required some kind of attention other than psychiatric treatment, and the forty-five per cent who *were* psychiatric cases needed some other kind of ministration in addition to medical help.)

What kind of help was required, either instead of or in addition to psychiatry? Was it possible that non-medical counselling might save at least some of those contemplating suicide?

In the summer of 1953, I had an opportunity to discover how useful, in some cases, such counselling could be. I had written an article for a magazine called *Picture*

Post, giving what I believed to be an enlightened, Christian philosophy of sex. The correspondence which this provoked kept me busy for several weeks, almost all the letters being from people who had been troubled about some sexual problem, often for years, and had not found any one in whom they felt they could confide without fear of condemnation. Exactly a hundred of these letters arrived the day after the publication of the article, and out of these, fourteen were written by people who appeared to be so much in agony of mind about their sexual problems that they were on the verge of suicide. The remarkable thing was that only one of these needed to be referred to a psychiatrist: the other thirteen (one of whom had in the past had some psychiatric attention) were able to be helped, apparently satisfactorily, by straightforward counselling, in most cases without explicit religious content. It is impossible to guess how many of the remaining eighty-six out of these first hundred correspondents might have become suicidal if they had not found someone with whom to discuss their problems acceptably. Out of a total of 235 persons who wrote as a result of that article, two dozen appeared to be suicidal, three of whom I advised to seek medical help. It is interesting that this proportion, one in eight, has continued to be roughly the proportion of the serious cases coming to The Samaritans referred for psychiatric treatment. I am not, of course, suggesting that only twelve and a half per cent of potential suicides need psychiatry more urgently than they need anything else: the potential suicides who seek the help of The Samaritans are clearly not typical of the whole range of potential suicides, and it is not surprising that the

19

majority of those who need psychiatry seek it without coming to The Samaritans first.

Once I was reasonably certain that non-medical counselling had *some* contribution to make, however small, towards the prevention of suicide, I felt a clear duty to take steps to try to provide this for all who might be persuaded to apply for it. But how was such counselling to be made available, and its existence brought to the attention of those who might benefit from it? There was no way of knowing who the potential suicides were, so the only way they could be informed of the existence of an emergency service specially for them, was by informing everybody; and the only practical way of informing everybody was through the good offices of the Press (and later of radio and television).

The first necessity, however, was time to operate such a service, a base from which to operate, and an income on which to live while doing it. A church in the City of London, where there are hardly any parochial responsibilities because of the lack of resident population, was the obvious answer. Out of the blue I received the offer of the Lord Mayor's Parish Church of St. Stephen Walbrook, from the Patrons, the Worshipful Company of Grocers, who subsequently appointed me Rector because, having had my scheme explained to them, they wished the experiment to be tried. (Eleven years later, the Worshipful Company showed their satisfaction with the results of that experiment by paying the cost of the conversion of the crypt of the church into premises from which The Samaritans could continue to operate, whoever might subsequently hold the position of Rector.)

The idea of an emergency service automatically brought to mind the telephone, on the dial of which appear the words: "Emergency calls—for police, fire, ambulance dial 999." Citizens have long been accustomed to make for the telephone in an emergency, but the 999 system did not cater for those whose emergency was not that their house had been burgled or caught fire, or they themselves physically injured in some accident, but that they were in such despair that they were contemplating self-destruction. There seemed no good reason why there should not be a fourth emergency service, for potential suicides; but in the experimental stage it could clearly not be a nationwide addition to the 999 system. The telephone at St. Stephen Walbrook was bound to be on the Mansion House exchange, so either 9999 or 9000 would be sufficiently reminiscent of 999 for the proposed pilot emergency number. In 1953 the repair of the church after its severe damage in the blitz was almost complete and the contractors had had the telephone reconnected. It was covered with dust when I used it to enquire whether the number could be changed to MANsion House 9000. The operator replied that someone would be certain already to have such a desirable number, but she would make enquiries if I would tell her the number I was speaking from. I wiped the dust from the dial, and told her not to bother: St. Stephen Walbrook already had the coveted number.

There was now a willing man with a base and an income and an emergency telephone with an easily memorized number. All that was required was for the Press to make that number widely known and for me to try to cope with what happened as a result. I had for years had to earn my living in Fleet Street because my income was only sufficient to pay my secretary, so I had no difficulty in interesting the Press in such a 'human interest story' as the provision of an emergency telephone for potential suicides, and thousands of pounds' worth of free publicity for the scheme was willingly given, not only in the early days when it was 'news', but regularly over the years. (In 1965, press cuttings from all over the country come in at the rate of about a dozen a day.)

As soon as MANsion House 9000 was publicized, it began to be used, and mostly by people who could benefit to some extent from the counselling offered. Two things quickly became clear: first, that for most 'clients' the telephone was only a convenient means of emergency contact requiring a minimum of effort and allowing anonymity to be maintained until confidence had been established, when in almost all cases the client wished to come for a face-to-face interview; and secondly, that no one man, however devoted and efficient his secretary, could possibly meet the need of all the people who sought help, even when the service was new and the majority of potential clients had never heard of it. It was by no means unusual in those early days for me to have a succession of eleven one-hour interviews with old and new clients, constantly interrupted by telephone calls, with no time to go out for meals or even to write letters or make telephone calls at the request of clients.

Fortunately, however, the publicity attracted offers of help as well as clients. Some of these offers turned out to be from people *needing* help, some from cranks, and some from would-be Lady Bountifuls or evangelizers, but one or two from professionals willing to help by having clients referred to them, and some from good-hearted people who genuinely wanted to help humbly in any way they could.

It was by no means clear in what way good-hearted, unqualified, 'ordinary' people could help potential suicides, except indirectly by ministering to, and running errands for, me while I tried to cope single-handed with the results of a very rash offer. It was they, not I, who discovered how they could help. They turned up regularly, and sat around in the outer vestry while I interviewed clients in the inner vestry, and, being the type of people they were, they did not allow clients waiting their turn to twiddle their thumbs, sit staring vacantly into space, or sob quietly in a corner, unless this was what the client wanted to do. The lay volunteers engaged the clients in conversation, plied them with coffee and cigarettes, and generally made them feel at home. Three things began to happen whose significance was not immediately noticed. First, counselling began to go much better. Clients were not merely free of the exasperation which comes from long and tedious waiting, but were in a calmly receptive state of mind and had had their confidence in me, as the person doing the counselling, enormously built up. Secondly, a proportion of the clients went away happily without having had any counselling at all, having found all that they needed in the ministrations of the lay volunteers. This seemed to apply particularly to clients who on arrival had proclaimed in no uncertain terms that they wanted to see the Rector personally and were not going to be fobbed off with anybody else. Thirdly, the failures of my counselling were almost always picked up by the volunteers as the client passed through the outer vestry on the way out. The majority of these clients were psychotic, and therefore not amenable to counselling, but in a great number of cases were able to appreciate kindly interest and to benefit from the supportive friendship of volunteers who were determined to do something useful and were not afraid of making the situation worse, because it clearly could not *be* worse. Like the cheerful ward maid who makes friends with a patient in the closed ward of a mental hospital, blissfully ignorant of the fact that he is the most dangerous patient they have ever had, these volunteers were angels who rushed in where fools fear to tread. They were not all equally good, of course, and some fell by the wayside, but the best of them remained, and it is to them rather than to myself that The Samaritans owes its origin. The *Daily Mirror* had published a story under the optimistic headline "Samaritan Priest Will Save Suicides": it was only a few months before it became evident that the word "Samaritan" needed to be put in the plural, and the word "Priest" dropped. From that moment (early in 1954) the original concept of a non-medical (but still professional) counselling service was abandoned, and its place was taken by the concept of a *befriending* service by lay volunteers, selected by, and operating under the supervision of, someone who was capable of supplementing their efforts by counselling the clients or by referring them for treatment when necessary, but who would never again pick up the emergency telephone or receive a client on arrival if there were a Samaritan available to do this.

An example of befriending effecting what neither treatment nor counselling can achieve is a woman whose diagnosis was paranoid schizophrenia and who was discharged from hospital when there was no further improvement in her condition but she was judged not to be dangerous. Her husband would not have her back (we have had several such cases, some involving another woman and some not—I will not say which this was, lest one of them should imagine she can identify herself, and then perhaps start thinking other people could). She was very lonely, and unlikely to be able to make friends because she was a great bore and also very suspicious and touchy. She came to us for help in getting a job—one of a great number whose presenting problem is not their main one. She was at that time quite unemployable, and if we had persuaded anyone to take her on they would never have helped us in this way again. The muddle she made of the occasional jobs she found for herself was fantastic; doubtless the firms concerned could afford it, but it was not doing *her* any good (except financially) to keep getting the sack with wages in lieu of notice. She was given a very patient and assiduous befriender, who spent countless hours with her over a period of years. There were many ups and downs, and at no stage could one speak of a 'cure', but the woman was able sometimes to hold down simple jobs for reasonable periods, and her life was much happier and her mental state improved. I could not have done what that befriender did—and not only because I have not as much free time.

Another case where befriending came to the rescue when all else failed was that of a man suffering from a severe depressive illness who flatly refused to see a doctor even though he agreed with me that only medical treatment could cure his depression. There were some indications that he had heard gruesome and misleading stories about electroplexy from a neighbour who knew someone who had had it; he called it "shock treatment", though there is no shock (even the convulsive effect is nowadays avoided by relaxant drugs), and stated that "over his dead body" would it be done to him. I told him it was for a doctor to decide what *kind* of treatment was necessary, and that without treatment there might well be a dead body on which no one would waste electricity or anti-depressant drugs. After an hour's debate, he agreed that treatment would not hurt him and would relieve his depression; and added that he would not have it at any price. He reminded me that I had stated in the paper that clients were as free to go as they were to come, and that if after talking with us they still wanted to commit suicide, we would make no effort to prevent them by force. I agreed that this was so, and asked if he would like a Samaritan to drive him home. I will not say whether or not he was the man who for some reason I never discovered was carrying an enormously heavy sewing-machine with him, but he accepted the lift, and I briefed the person I had chosen to be his befriender. This Samaritan never made any reference to treatment or to depression or to me, but concentrated on making friends with the client, who some weeks later (including a couple of anxious occasions when his friend sat up all night with him) asked to be taken to the doctor because he felt he ought not to go on being "such a burden" to his friend. (This client *did* have electroplexy and it cured him in about three weeks.)

Still another example of befriending being the real need was that of a young man who was painfully shy, and who wondered whether he might be homosexual since he never dared to address a girl and was tongue-tied if one addressed him. His only sexual experience (apart from standard adolescent masturbation, which, thanks to a wise clergyman who took his confirmation class, did not bother him) was years before, with another boy at school, who took the initiative. Such clients normally have at least a little counselling, but this one got swept into befriending at a busy period and by the time we got round to arranging it, it was clear he did not need it. His befriender refused to regard the problem as one of homosexuality, on the ground that the young man was equally shy with both sexes, and treated it simply as a problem of loneliness arising from lack of confidence (though if any complications had arisen he would of course have reported this, and some counselling would have been arranged). The befriender took the client with him to all sorts of functions where young people of both sexes were to be found, drew him out, saw to it that he was included in any conversation, made openings for him to tell an anecdote which the be-friender had previously extracted from him and found entertaining; and so on. After a few weeks of this the client really began to hold his own in company, though he would never, mercifully, become 'the life and soul of the party'. A few months later, the client had found a girlfriend, and the Samaritan withdrew, having been instrumental in completely transforming the client's life. It was typical that when this volunteer was given a small pat on the back—a thing we rarely do—he muttered that he had not done anything, really. Nor had he: except be a Samaritan, meeting the client's simple need.

All these befrienders were content to be members of a body of lay people who, like the Samaritan in the parable, are moved with compassion by the desperate plight of their fellow men and women and who, lacking professional qualifications or competence, offer themselves and what they have to give, namely their personal concern, their time, attention and friendship. The Samaritan comes in all shapes and sizes, of all ages and both sexes, from all kinds of background, with all kinds of interests; and in a big enough collection to man an emergency telephone twenty-four hours a day, so there is sufficient variety to 'match' any client who comes looking for a real friend. The Samaritan listens, accepts, cares; and this can make all the difference between life and death for those who feel that no one has time for them, that they are rejected, and that nobody cares.

The Samaritans are all inspired by the same spirit. Even the most convinced unbeliever in the supernatural talks about 'spirit'. It is not necessary to believe in the Holy Spirit to use expressions like, "There is a good spirit in this school, office, or scout troop." It is not necessary to believe in a Personal Devil to use expressions like, "There was a bad spirit in the meeting, community, or mob." Whether one's thinking is theological or anti-theological, and whether one's attempts to formulate one's beliefs and a philosophy on which they rest make sense or not, it is an undeniable fact that there are movements or tendencies which affect people who are widely separated from one another so that ideas appear to be born or to meet an enthusiastic response in many different places at about the same time. It happens that the idea of an emergency telephone service for potential suicides started in my mind, but many other minds all over the world were moving in the same direction and only had to hear of my London experiment to know at once that this was what they had been groping after. In addition, all over the world there are people who are contracting out of the 'rat race' and looking for some way of serving their fellow human beings in a spirit of neighbourly kindliness. However powerful may be the hold of a selfish and materialistic spirit which expresses itself in the slogan, "I'm all right, Jack," not everyone has succumbed to this. In every street, if one could find them, are one or two people who are natural Samaritans; who are not anxious, like the Priest and the Levite, to pass by on the other side, and are not afraid of being involved.

In every age there have been some people who were, in the original warm sense of the word, 'charitable'. In previous centuries most 'good works' have been done by people of this kind. In our day, the State has more and more taken over the responsibility for the welfare of its citizens, and this is a right and necessary development; but it has left many men and women of goodwill with a feeling of frustration because there is so little that they can do for someone other than themselves which can compare with what professionally trained people can accomplish. To such people, The Samaritans, and other organizations which utilize the services of untrained volunteers, come as a godsend. To be able to make all the difference in the world to another human being is to find one's real self. People have grown accustomed to thinking of 'rescue' as something confined to doctors, ambulance men, firemen, lifeboat men, pit rescue squads and other specialized occupations—only by an unlikely chance would an ordinary citizen find himself in the position of being able to save a human life. Even if he *did* find himself in such a situation, he fears he would lack the skill or presence of mind to be able to intervene effectively. A child is drowning in the canal, and he has never learnt to swim; the victim of a motor accident is bleeding to death, and he cannot remember where the pressure points are; he wants to get someone out of a smoke-filled room, and does not know there is breathable air near the floor.

The person who does not *know* may fail in the rescue, or make the situation worse, or add himself to the number needing to be rescued. He will mostly be well advised to run and summon someone who is competent to cope with the particular situation.

The beauty of The Samaritans as an opportunity for life-saving service is that by its very nature it does not require difficult skills: it simply requires a particular type of person. Friends may be good, bad or indifferent, and so may neighbours; and the good ones are good because of what they are, not because of particular technical skills. Certain skills may make a person more *useful*: if the couple next door consist of a handyman who can mend anything and a woman who is good at all kinds of domestic emergencies, this will increase their usefulness in a particular kind of crisis, but unless they are neighbourly people, liking to be of service, they might as well be hamhanded and stupid for all the good it will do for those next door. Since the essence of neighbourliness is kindness and interest rather than the ability to do jobs for which one would normally have to pay, a good neighbour may be totally unskilled and yet add greatly to life's contentment.

The Samaritan volunteer is not accepted into the organization because he knows how to cope with someone who has taken an overdose, or because of his experience in getting people down off roofs and window-ledges from which they threaten to jump. He (or she) is chosen not for any particular abilities (useful though these may be, and some volunteers have them), but for those human qualities that make a good friend, a good neighbour, a good person to have with you if you are in trouble. It is not so much by what he does, but by *being* his own patient, tolerant, interested self, that the Samaritan helps clients most. Someone can always be found to do the things that require particular knowledge or abilities, and the Samaritan is prepared to go to endless trouble to do this, but he knows that his talent for friendship, and his unfailing concern, are what he was engaged for, and that this is the thing the majority of the clients most need.

Naturally, the befriending of people who may be very disturbed is itself a skill which needs to be learned, but it can only be learned by those who already possess the human qualities which make them Samaritans. What friendship *is*, and how it is most suitably manifested in a particular situation, is something which comes both from instruction and discussion, and from experience. It is not enough to be kindly and well-meaning, but just as those who have a good ear and a love of music can usually be taught to play different instruments, so the Samaritan type of person has a natural understanding and appreciation of the things which are explained in the Preparation Classes and the Case Conferences, and constantly learns both from his own experience and from observation of his colleagues in their dealings with clients. It does not happen that Samaritan types with few educational or intellectual advantages find that they cannot master all the psychology and other highfalutin subjects which are discussed: the subjects do not appear to be difficult, if they are presented in a Samaritan context, because the volunteer has a feeling for human relationships and even the most unexpected revelations of the peculiar ways in which the mind can work are of fascinating interest to those who want to do their best for other human beings in abnormal mental or emotional states: they are grasped almost intuitively. The instruction might not be remembered, and it might not be possible for the person to reproduce it, but it will modify his practice and will become a part of his manner of dealing with clients with the same lack of conscious application that one shows in riding a bicycle once one has got the knack. Just as a bright boy with an interest in mathematics will find the first steps in calculus fascinating and easy, so the natural Samaritan finds no difficulty in learning, for instance, that clients suffering from paranoid delusions of persecution must not be argued with, because any attempt to deal with their irrational beliefs by rational argument merely forces them to use all their usually considerable ingenuity in defending their delusional system, which is thereby deepened and extended. A Samaritan may or may not remember the explanation of the reason for neither agreeing or dis-agreeing but in any case refusing to discuss the delusions and changing the subject to something on which the client thinks sanely, but his natural sympathy with the client's distress will express itself in ways which quite unconsciously are impeccable from a psychological point of view, and over a period of befriending of such a client the Samaritan may well have built up and increased the sane areas of the client's thinking and his or her healthy interests. Indeed, there are some Samaritans who seem to know without being told how to deal with any kind of person whatever: their natural gentleness, consideration, good manners and gracious-ness lead them safely past many pitfalls into which others of us might fall. But most Samaritans owe a great deal to the instruction they receive, and would be the first to admit that even sanctified commonsense is not always enough.

All the Preparation Classes are about befriending: what it is, how it differs from counselling, what effects it has in particular cases, how it is best expressed in relation to particular psychological, sexual or spiritual problems, how it assists whatever counselling may also be undertaken for a client, how it can help clients to benefit from any medical treatment they may be re-ceiving, what types of person cannot benefit from it at all, and what types can benefit so little that they are not really 'up The Samaritans' street'. During the Preparation Classes, the new volunteer not only learns a great deal that will be useful in the work but is also very likely to manifest any attitudes which would make him or her unsuitable for acceptance. The greatest amount is learned afterwards in practice, and Continuation Classes are able to go much more deeply into the big question of how to befriend, because problems which were academic in the Preparation Classes are now ones which have actually been encountered by the volunteer in the course of his duties. The most important lessons of all, however, are learned by close association with those who are most truly Samaritans, and whose attitudes communicate themselves to those of the newer volunteers who are prepared to be influenced by their example. 'How to be a Samaritan' is not something that was laid down by the founder of the organization, but something which has been displayed in living actuality by a succession of dedicated volunteers whose communal personality is now 'The Samaritans'.

When applicants emerge from the Preparation Classes, they go on 'Observation Duty', which not only permits them to observe what goes on, but also allows them to be observed by experienced Samaritans. The new volunteers start in the lowest of the three grades into which volunteers are divided, because at this stage the organization is not quite sure what they have in them and how close they are able to come to the pattern of the ideal Samaritan. As soon as it appears reasonably likely that they have some Samaritan qualities, and are also still keen, they are promoted to the second grade, where the majority of them will remain indefinitely. In some situations they appear to be Samaritans, in others they appear to lack something, but on the whole they make a valuable contribution, and their readiness to continue serving humbly in the middle grade is itself a good sign. From amongst them, a few are selected for the highest category, and admitted to 'The Company of Samaritans'. These are people who are judged to be natural Samaritans who can be depended upon to act as Samaritans in all circumstances and at all times. In each Branch, the first ones (there were six in the original London Branch) have to be chosen by the person in charge of the Branch, because there is no one else to do it, and these form the nucleus around which 'The Company of Samaritans' grows. Once formed, the 'Company' (not to be confused with the Limited Company which the whole Association technically is, though it is not called so) adds to its numbers by unanimous election by its existing members. In very large branches, where it is hardly possible for each Samaritan to know all the other volunteers sufficiently well, 'unanimous' comes to mean something more like '*nem. con.*' though even here a person proposed would only be elected if he or she had widespread support and the other members would trust the judgment of the proposers on the basis of their own knowledge of them and the discussion of the candidate's qualities which would take place. Very high standards are demanded by the Company before any volunteer is elected to membership of it. Although election does not depend on the amount of activity, and has nothing whatever to do with seniority, a certain minimum amount of time given to the organization is required; but the chief consideration is always whether in the judgment of the Company the candidate *is* undoubtedly a Samaritan. One who is elected will have been judged to be loving and wise, charitable rather than sentimental, neither hard nor soft, utterly discreet and loyal, sufficiently humble to be surprised at being elected, but accepting the decision realistically and without question, sufficiently conscientious to 'reclassify' himself or herself in case of any failure to maintain the standard or because changed circumstances interfere with the work, and so devoted to the Company that if all the rest were to be travelling on a chartered 'plane that crashed, the one remaining would build it up again from the beginning.

People of this calibre are few and far between, but they do exist, and they exist in all walks of life and from all kinds of backgrounds. They are found in all branches of the Christian church and amongst adherents of the non-Christian faiths, and they are also found amongst agnostics and humanists. They have more in common with one another than they have with other members of their own group who are not Samaritans. It may rightly be supposed that the fellowship they develop amongst themselves is of a rare and precious quality, and that they become even more truly Samaritans by their association with one another. At their meetings, which no one else is permitted to attend except the person in charge of their Branch, who presides, they never take a vote: it would be unthinkable for a majority to impose its will on the minority. They continue their discussion, "speaking the truth in love", until they arrive at a common mind, which the person in charge has the duty of expressing. If even one member finds himself or herself unable to agree, no decision is made. In particular no one is added to the Company if one of its existing members is even a little doubtful whether the person proposed is truly a Samaritan. It is realized that any volunteer in the 'middle grade' who was disappointed or lost interest at not being elected a Companion would not deserve a place even in the 'middle grade', where every opportunity of serving the clients which a Companion enjoys is available to him. The only thing a Companion does which other volunteers do not do as a rule is to take charge of a duty, and since Samaritan Companions are the least bossy people imaginable, uninterested in power and authority, they are the right people to be in charge, though they constantly have to force themselves, against the grain, to control the activities of their fellow-volunteers. It is entirely in the spirit of the organization that power-seekers are severely discouraged and authority exercised by those who desire it least. Naturally the Companions are given all the most difficult tasks and are as a matter of course treated with the least consideration. 'Helpers' are likely to be approached in some such terms as, "I wonder if it would be convenient for you to . . ." And even to Members (the 'middle grade') one usually says, "please," or, "I want you to . . ." But to Companions the person in charge would say, "Go to such and such a place and do so-and-so." If for any reason he or she were unable to comply, it would be the Companion who would apologize not the one who was issuing the urgent instruction.

The heart of any Branch organized on the same pattern as the London Branch, once it has passed its own Probationary period and become a full voting member of the Association, is its 'Company of Samaritans'. It is this Company which does the real work of the organization. Consultants exist in order to supplement its activities; Leaders are there in order to provide the professional supervision the Company needs; and the other volunteers are there to assist the Company in its work and to provide a recruiting ground. The other four categories of membership are all dispensable: only as long as there is a Company of Samaritans can the branch be said to exist as it was meant to be. Leaders may come and go, as may Consultants; other volunteers may prove unsuitable or lose interest; but the Company goes on. No one ever leaves the Company unless through sickness or removal he finds it necessary to reclassify. The effective working of a branch depends upon the Company of Samaritans, for if the Samaritans do not know who is a Samaritan and who is not, or who merely *might* be, who does know? The people who are most concerned with the welfare of the clients are the ones who are most determined that the soul of the movement shall be embodied in the best examples of Samaritans that can be found. Some people, of course, do not like the idea of the Company, saying that it is invidious to differentiate among the volunteers. It would be invidious in worldly organizations which have to take account of seniority, efficiency and other false gods. In the work of the Samaritans, it is essential to 'differentiate', and the only question is whether this should be done publicly or privately. There are some people who can be entrusted with any client, however difficult; others who are beginners, just feeling their feet; and others who can manage moderately difficult relationships with clients reasonably well. The person responsible for deploying the members to the best possible advantage of the client *must* have at least three 'grades' in his mind, and the advantage of having them not in a secret book, but in a published list issued to all volunteers is that it is clear who should be approached in particular circumstances, what kind of person the organization is really looking for, and who is to be put in charge of periods of duty. The biggest advantage, however, is the possibility of a Company of Samaritans, whose life and spirit are the life and spirit of the whole organization. The Company is an exclusive club in the sense that there is no way of getting into it except by unanimous election by the existing members. It is not exclusive in the sense that an increase in its membership is not desired, or in the sense that the members swagger or throw their weight about. Admission cannot be gained by money, or influence or wire-pulling, and not even by frantic activity in the work of the organization. Volunteers in the organization go quietly on with their work without worrying about 'promotion', and those who *are* in the fullest sense Samaritans may be recognized as such, and, if so, will be elected to the Company, and, if not, will continue to work equally devotedly in the 'middle grade'. Not the least of the advantages of this arrangement is that aggressive, self-important, committee-minded or power-seeking individuals, who are not wanted in the organization anyway, quickly realize that it is an organization in which they will not get very far.

It may seem odd, after all that I have written about the centrality of the 'Company of Samaritans', that the Council of Management of the Association should, in July 1965, have unanimously decided, on my suggestion, approved by the Executive Committee, that the third category of volunteers should be optional, and that even where it is used, its members need not necessarily form a self-perpetuating Company of Samaritans. The reason for this is that the needs of the clients dictate that existing Branches of The Samaritans should continue to operate as constituent parts of the Association provided they do not transgress our few unalterable principles, and enquiry showed that it was an indisputable fact that four variations on the original pattern had emerged. If these variants had clearly prevented the Branches in question from operating effectively as Samaritan Branches, the Association would have had no hesitation in requiring changes on pain of expulsion: but this was not the case. Samaritan work was undeniably being done in a 'Samaritan' spirit in Branches whose organization differed in some respects from that of the original model, and once the Association had had time to become an entity, it seemed right to legitimize those variants which worked well rather than to attempt to secure uniformity for its own sake. The very first centre in the United Kingdom outside London (Edinburgh) had from the beginning been under the control of a Committee instead of a Director, and all the Scottish Branches except Dundee had followed suit. Since of the twenty-one centres which banded together in 1963 to form the Association, three of the six oldest were Scottish, the 'Committee system' was recognized as a valid one from the outset, and the policy of accepting local traditions where possible, whilst avoiding their uncontrolled proliferation in the future, has continued.

Probationary Branches have never been permitted to have a 'Company of Samaritans' until they achieved full membership of the Association, and so it seemed reasonable that smaller Branches, which represented that they did not need a third category of volunteers, should be free to continue without it.

Some Branches wanted to call all their members 'Samaritans', instead of reserving this name for members of a Company of Samaritans and describing the other two categories as 'Helpers' and 'Probationers'; and this commended itself so strongly to the Executive and the Council that they have decided that all members of the Association, including Leaders and Consultants, should be termed 'Samaritans', and their other descriptions be prefixed by 'Samaritan' used as an adjective. Now that this has been passed by the Council of Management, I am very proud to become entitled to be called a Samaritan again—a designation I lost ten years ago when it was decided that parsons and doctors could only be Directors or Consultants.

One or two Branches wished to have a third category of volunteers to use in a supervisory capacity but wished to have them chosen by their Committee instead of by a self-perpetuating Company of Samaritans.

The Council of Management has now resolved (a) that all members shall be called 'Samaritans'; (b) that in all Branches the volunteers shall serve for a probationary period as Samaritan Helpers before being classified as Samaritan Members; (c) that in those Branches which choose to have a third category of volunteers they shall be called Samaritan Companions if they are members of a Company of Samaritans which elects its own members, and Samaritan Supervisors if they are appointed by a Committee; (d) that the classification Samaritan Leaders shall include not only Directors and Deputy Directors, but also lay Leaders who may make the third category of volunteers unnecessary in Branches with a number of Committee members and other such Leaders; and (e) that the classification Samaritan Consultant shall be used for persons attached to the Branch in an advisory capacity.

Volunteers engage in Befriending and Interviewing: they are not employed in Counselling, unless in exceptional cases they have qualifications for this. Counselling is done by Leaders and Consultants; but the chief function of the Leaders is to select, instruct, and supervise the volunteers, making sure that they are not left with the burden of making, themselves, decisions that they are not competent to make, and that they do not become anxious about those entrusted to them to befriend.

The whole atmosphere of The Samaritans is *sui generis*. Most of the standards of the world are rejected. Just as in an internment camp—another instance of people being together up against the harsh realities of life and death—nothing is important except the humanity of each person, for those who have money cannot get at it, those who have fine clothes at home are in the same rags as everyone else, all eat the same food and either share or do not share with the weak and the sick, so in The Samaritans nobody is interested in your money or title or accent or the importance of your job, but only in whether you are a person whom merely to be with will make the clients feel hopeful again. Your religion (or lack of it), your political affiliations and other irrelevant matters will not be mentioned to the clients, and your colleagues are unlikely to discover about these, except by chance, because you will have more important things to talk with them about. Somewhere buried in the files is your application form, on which your religion, if any, is mentioned, only because it might happen that a client wished to speak with someone of the same faith as himself. In that case, someone would have to look it up. Proselytizing is strictly forbidden: hardly ever does a client want to be evangelized, and although all human beings have needs that may be described as 'spiritual', these are not met by trotting out ready-made answers to questions that have not been asked.

The Samaritans is not a church organization, nor even an exclusively Christian organization: it comprises amongst its membership people of all faiths and of no explicit faith, and whilst in a nominally Christian country the majority are Christians of one sort or another, this is not true of its membership in other countries. The fact that its name and its inspiration come from a parable in the Christian Gospel is of less significance than the fact that that particular parable appeals deeply to all men and women of goodwill everywhere, no matter what religion they may profess or fail to profess. In England, quite a number of branches have their headquarters in Church premises, because it is essential that they should be situated in the centre of large cities where office accommodation is expensive and the Vestry or Hall of a church is usually the most economical form that office accommodation can take in the most expensive part of a big town. Clients do not seem to be deterred from coming to church premises, although the vast majority of them are not churchgoers: what the Samaritans offer has been made sufficiently clear sufficiently often for clients to know that even if at some stage they find themselves talking to a man wearing a dog-collar, the purpose of that encounter will be in order that he may help them with his specialized knowledge of some problem that is troubling them. The vast majority of Samaritan Directors are clergymen, and this is because of all the professions other than the medical profession, which can only be used in a consultative capacity in a non-medical organization, the profession of 'Minister of Religion' is the one which lends itself best to the type of work a Director has to do. This is not to say that all clergymen and ministers would be suitable for running a Samaritan Branch: many are too rigid or too ecclesiastical, or feel themselves to be called to a definitely evangelistic or pastoral ministry. It is noteworthy that those clergy and ministers who *do* feel called to serve as Samaritan Directors, and are found suitable for the work, are very much of one mind, irrespective of the denomination from which they come. The fellowship, transcending denominational and other barriers, which exists among the volunteers is also found at Directors' Conferences. Indeed, the question has been asked 'is the coming Great Church already to be seen in embryo in The Samaritans?' The question does not imply that ecumenical activity is part of the function of the organization, but it points to the existence of a fellow-ship of service in which the members, each loyal to his or her own convictions and community, work together in harmony and mutual respect, learning humbly from one another and never seeking to score points off one another or pretending to have a monopoly of truth. Whilst those in authority in the various religious bodies rightly seek formally for reunion, ordinary people from the rank and file are already enjoying the kind of fellowship without which any reunion would be a mere outward form.

What happens when a client rings up?

Whether by day or by night, whether in a large or small branch, what is aimed at is that the person who answers the telephone when a client rings shall be a volunteer, i.e., a fellow human being who cares. Even in the London branch, which has a full-time staff during office hours, Monday to Friday, the emergency tele-phone is always answered by a volunteer. Some of the smaller branches have difficulty in finding sufficient volunteers to man the telephone during working hours, and are therefore compelled to use Leaders for this purpose, but generally speaking a client expects that when he telephones he will be answered by a Samaritan, not by a parson, doctor, social worker or other expert, and his expectation is seldom disappointed. The volun-teer who answers the telephone does not attempt to obtain all the information about the client and his problem in detailed form in order to 'solve' the problem. He is content to listen, to be sympathetic, and to make the client feel that he or she is personally interested in the client's well-being and concerned about the client's unhappiness.

Naturally, in most cases a good deal of information is given and is entered in the Log Book. If it is sufficiently full, a Report Form will be filled up; otherwise this Form will wait until a proper interview has been done.

The main purpose of the first conversation on the telephone is to win the client's confidence and persuade him or her to come and be seen face to face. Those clients who wish to remain anonymous voices on the telephone may do so, but only one in twenty make this decision, and some of those later change their mind and decide to trust The Samaritans with their identity and their address, knowing that no use will be made of this information without their permission. If the call is during the night, and the client cannot be invited to come to the office, if it is essential to see someone at once a volunteer (not one who is tied to the telephone by being on Night Watch) will be sent to him. Whether the volunteer goes alone or with others (in Edinburgh each such volunteer has a romantically-named 'Night Partner'), this is described as 'Flying Squad', and it is odd that the more dangerous the area covered (Soho, for example) the more likely it is that the 'Squad' will be one apparently frail but intrepid woman. Flying Squad may not be called out by Night Watch without permission from 'Home Service', which means the Director or other Leader on duty by his home telephone that night.

Sooner or later, in the office or elsewhere, the client almost always meets a Samaritan or a Leader, and in the course of an interview lasting about an hour the facts of the situation will be ascertained and will be incorporated in a report on a standard form. This interview will be conducted by the most experienced volunteer present, unless the one in charge decides that the client is probably a scrounger on whom a novice can practice interviewing and filling up a Report Form under supervision.

The person whose duty it is will read this report fairly soon afterwards, and make a decision what is to be done to help the client and who is to do it. Whatever else is prescribed, in almost all cases someone will be allocated to befriend the client. If counselling is necessary, an appointment will be made for this in addition to the befriending, and if the client needs to see a doctor, and is willing to do so, arrangements for this will be made. In any case, a responsible person will be in charge of that particular client, and will arrange and supervise whatever befriending and other ministrations he is to have. The volunteer doing the befriending keeps in regular touch with the person in charge of the case and works under his direction. The majority of clients have at least some counselling, but the people who do this would be the first to admit that the greatest benefits are received through the befriending done by the volunteers.

The purpose of befriending is not to remain in this relationship for the rest of the client's life. It could be said that the purpose of befriending is to make itself unnecessary, by bringing out those potentialities for good human relationships in the client which at the time he first came were not in evidence. Befriending continues as long as the person in charge considers that it will be beneficial to the client, and, if it is successfully done, sooner or later the client will be able to make his or her own friends and the Samaritan befriender can be withdrawn and allocated to someone else. The Samaritans exist to deal with the acute crises in people's lives, not in order to give lifetime support to the chronically inadequate. This is not because the chronically inadequate do not need befriending, but because the kind of befriending from which they can benefit is different from the kind offered by the Samaritans, who are geared to deal with emergencies and think in terms of contact with a client for weeks and months rather than years. The befriending of the chronically inadequate, which may produce one per cent improvement per annum in some cases, needs to be done by a reasonably near neighbour, and it ought not to be too much to expect that Christian and other congregations should take responsibility for the chronically inadequate in their neighbourhood, whose befriending will often involve frequent contact with welfare services and can be done under the guidance of trained people. At present, many who fall into this category take up a great deal of additional time with welfare workers because they look to *them* for the befriending which they are not receiving in their own neighbourhood.

An organization dedicated to the prevention of suicide must not dissipate its energies by widening its terms of reference to such an extent as to impair the service it is offering in its chosen field. The entire human resources of many branches could be used up by a hundred inadequate personalities bordering on the psychopathic, only a handful of whom would ever be suicide risks. Just as in a railway accident rescue workers would concentrate on those who were severely injured and possibly bleeding to death, leaving people with sprains and bruises to less skilled people, so the Samaritans, who have been assembled in order to deal as much as possible with matters of life and death, dare not let themselves be bogged down with other matters which people who have not been mobilized for this urgent task can deal with equally well.

If they are to fulfil their purpose, Samaritans must not be sentimental, but realistic. They would be failing in their duty if they were to adopt some such slogan as 'No one is ever turned away'. If hysterical and aggressive psychopaths were not turned away, no one else would ever get any attention. If purely welfare cases were not referred to the appropriate organization which exists to help them, The Samaritans would become an amateur and inefficient casework agency and thus fail to make their own unique contribution. If Samaritans attempted to do badly what specialist organizations do well, instead of enjoying the goodwill and co-operation of these, they would be regarded by them with justifiable suspicion. It is difficult enough that some clients insist on having, for example, their marital counselling from members of The Samaritans, refusing to be referred to a Marriage Guidance Council—not that this body would claim any monopoly of marriage guidance, which has long been performed by the clergy and others, but it is clearly desirable that The Samaritans should be seen not as a rival to any existing service but as providing a service which but for them would not exist. One of the reasons for the rapid spread and growth of the movement is that there was a desperate need which was not entirely or exactly being met.

Naturally, it is not possible for the Samaritans to confine their activities exclusively to those who are in imminent danger of taking their own life. Just as a considerable number of applicants to join the organization has to be 'processed' in order to discover first the possibles, then the probables, then the ones who are to the best of our judgment certainties, so a considerable number of clients have to be dealt with in order to ensure that amongst them there are some who might, and some who would, have killed themselves if The Samaritans had not been there to help them. That is why our letter heading says "The Samaritans—to help those tempted to suicide or despair". No one who is feeling desperate need hesitate to get in touch with The Samaritans because he cannot lay his hand on his heart and swear an affidavit that he is on the point of killing himself. It is sufficient for The Samaritans that he is very distressed: he does not need to threaten or attempt suicide in order to persuade them to take his situation to heart. But there is all the difference in the world between those who are in such a state that it would not be surprising if they were weary of life and whose situation can be transformed by the ministrations of The Samaritans, and those who are unfortunately unable to benefit from the kind of help the Samaritans offer and go round in many cases from one agency to another not seriously wanting or being capable of any real improvement.

The proportion of 'serious suicide risks' varies in different branches of The Samaritans between three and forty per cent of the clients: the average being about ten per cent. Something like twenty per cent are in a situation where they *might* commit suicide sooner or later unless something is done *now*; and there are also some who are very unhappy indeed but who, for conscientious reasons, would never make a suicidal act. In addition, there is a varying proportion of more or less 'inadequate' people who come to The Samaritans in times of crisis which recur at intervals, and who seem to benefit to some extent from periodical attention. No branch, however, can perform its task effectively if it allows the time and energies of its members to be taken up interminably by people who have come to 'the wrong shop', and the army of chronic scroungers and unrepentant confidence tricksters is as much out of place in a Samaritan centre as would be a ward-full of patients suffering from senile dementia—not because there is nothing that these people need, but because what they need is something the Samaritans are not organized to supply.

Unless it is clear from the outset that a person is grossly psychopathic, or has obviously misunderstood the nature of the organization, a decision whether The Samaritans can help or not is made only when the situation has become clear; and it comparatively rarely happens that a client has to be told that there is nothing further that The Samaritans can usefully do. Even in these cases it may be that some small service is performed by the Samaritans bearing the resentment and abuse which are sometimes vented on them, and which are a

very understandable expression of a person's frustration, especially if he is immature, or implacably unwilling to co-operate in his own interests. It sometimes happens that someone who has left in a rage because it just is not possible or desirable to comply with his demands, comes back in a more amenable frame of mind because nobody has held it against him that he was being 'difficult' or rude.

The vast majority of those who apply to The Samaritans for help are fortunately people whose situation the Samaritans are able to ameliorate, and for a not inconsiderable number Samaritan help has made all the difference between living and dying. The proportion of clients applying to a particular Samaritan Branch depends to a great extent on the amount of publicity which has been received by the Branch at that period. Those Branches which use posters or paid advertisements have, of course, control over the material, and in the case of radio and television programmes, which are usually pre-recorded, it is possible to ensure roughly the kind of presentation the organization desires. In the case of Press or magazine publicity, interviews are freely granted to reporters and agencies, and there is often no control over the use made of the material supplied. Thus, however carefully the interviewee may have expressed himself, a somewhat misleading impression may be given, either by the emphasis on what seems more sensational and the suppression of the rest, or by cuts made in an otherwise balanced story. There seems to be no way of avoiding this, and the movement has been most fortunate in having almost invariably the goodwill and co-operation of newspaper men. If, however, a Press report fails to make it clear that the whole service is confidential and that the client remains in charge of his or her own destiny, some clients will be deterred from making an approach; and if the kind of help The Samaritans do *not* offer, such as financial help, is mentioned, the number of clients asking for money or writing begging letters is enormously increased. The fault is by no means always with reporters and sub-editors when this kind of thing has happened: it requires a certain experience to *be* interviewed successfully by the Press, and beginners have sometimes said things they did not mean or failed to make themselves clear. It is in order to avoid this kind of difficulty that Press enquiries are always referred to the leadership, and volunteers are not allowed to give interviews unless these are arranged by the Director. The movement owes a great debt of gratitude to the Press for keeping the work of The Samaritans fairly regularly before the public, even though the nature of the work makes it impossible to give to the Press those 'case histories' which would make a story really interesting from their point of view, but which would deter clients from coming because of the fear that some such 'case history', unless in the most general terms, might be recognized by their friends and applied to themselves.

Newspaper men generally know their job, and the best of them have written stories far better than any we could have written for ourselves. If sometimes we have been a little squeamish about the way things were put, that did not really matter as long as the story was effective in bringing in clients. For instance, a well-written article in a London evening paper was given a headline (not by the writer of it) which made me squirm because I thought it vulgar. It appeared over a photograph of me, and ran, "The parson who can't be shocked." I felt very differently about it when large numbers of clients came along, most of them saying, "I have come to you because I'm told you can't be shocked." That was in the early days, when I saw almost all clients myself. A more recent successful headline refers to the volunteers, who do most of the work nowadays. It said, "They listen while people talk themselves out of trouble." We could not have put it better ourselves.

It is sometimes said that "there is no such thing as bad publicity"—that as long as people are talking about an organization or a product, it will help to make the organization known or sell the product, even if what is said is disparaging or inaccurate. I think this is usually true but that there are exceptions. A report in a local paper which gave the impression that although The Samaritans offered strict confidentiality to clients, if someone confessed to a crime the Samaritans' duty as citizens would take precedence over their undertaking to the organization, so that criminals would be handed over to the police, would have done the movement a great deal of harm if it had not been quickly scotched. People who have committed crimes of various kinds *are* amongst the clients of The Samaritans, and although they may be urged to give themselves up and face the music with a Samaritan by their side, they will in no circumstances be handed over or any information given about them without their consent. This is the only instance to my knowledge of publicity which could well have deterred many desperate clients from coming to The Samaritans, and in the end we hope it did no harm, because it enabled our firm principle of confidentiality to be reasserted in unmistakable terms.

The worst publicity I myself have ever had was from a national daily newspaper many years ago in connection with the death of a young man and his wife. The young man had come to me asking me to trace his wife and persuade her to return to him, as she had left without reason whilst their only child, little more than a baby, was ill in hospital. He flatly denied that there had been any quarrel or that he knew of any reason why she should have left without warning, and as she had no near relatives he had no idea where she could have gone. He wanted me to get the Sunday paper she always read to publish an appeal to her to return to him. Although he showed no signs of abnormality, experience of this work provides one with a kind of inner computer, which went click-click whirr-whirr, and I heard myself say, "No, I will not ask your wife to return to *you*, but I will see if I can persuade them to ask her to come and see *me*." He accepted this as being better than nothing, and proceeded to tell me that his wife might be mentally ill, because a fortnight earlier she had got up in the night and turned on the gas taps, and he had fortunately woken and turned them off again. He still insisted that she was not unhappy with him and that there were no disputes between them, and could offer no explanation for this attempt to kill herself and him. The more I thought about it after he had gone, the less I liked it. His story *could* be true, but it seemed far more likely that all was not well with the marriage, and that the true explanation both of the incident with the gas taps, if it happened at all, and the young woman's sudden departure at a time when her baby was ill in hospital, was that the husband was madly jealous and possessive, which, as I thought back on the interview, I could imagine him being. I became very anxious to see the young woman and to make sure that she was in no danger before making any arrangements for her to be reunited with her husband. I rang up the Sunday paper she always read, and was told that they did not publish that kind of appeal or there would be no room for anything else in the paper; but I was importunate, and eventually was put on to someone who said they would not do it for anyone else but they would do it for me. The appeal duly appeared, and must have been read by the young woman. Unfortunately, she did not come to see me before going home. The following day, she and her husband were both dead, of coal gas poisoning. If she had even telephoned me before going home, I should have been able to persuade her not to do so. Because of my appeal in the Sunday paper to her the police were anxious to know from me who killed whom. I replied that we should never know, but that my own opinion was that *he* was the one who had turned on the gas, because he was the one who "couldn't live without her", whilst she had been able to leave him and there was no evidence that she would have come back if she had not been anxious about her baby. I was later told that she had in fact spoken to a neighbour on the way home, saying that she was going to come and see me but first wanted to see how her husband was because she had been worried about his mental state—he had turned on the gas taps a fortnight before, she said, and she had fortunately woken and got up and turned them off.

The death of this young couple was distressing enough, and a number of newspapers rang up and discussed the matter with me, and gave accurate reports on the basis of the little I felt able to say. A woman reporter working for a national daily newspaper, however, nagged at me to try to get me to say that I felt guilty and had been responsible for the deaths of these two young people. Time and time again I told her that I did not feel guilty, and that if the young woman had done what I appealed to her to do, she and her husband would both now be alive. The reporter must have written her story before she rang me up, because it appeared under the headline, "Samaritan Rector: I Feel Guilty", with the sub-head, "If it had not been for me, this couple would now be alive." But even this barefaced lie and this monstrously unjust judgment did not, in the end, do The Samaritans the harm I had feared. First, protests to the paper eventually brought an assurance that instructions had been given that the Samaritans were to be reported more sympathetically in the future, and secondly, a large number of people wrote to say that I ought not to have felt guilty because I had done my best, and if the young woman had done as I asked she would have been saved. (There were even some who, thinking I *had* appealed to her to go back to her husband, still thought I had done the right thing and ought not to reproach myself!) Thirdly, a considerable number of clients came to see me, saying with unconscious irony that they hoped I would be willing to take as much trouble for them as I had for that young couple (though presumably not hoping for the same result). I never heard whether the woman reporter was rebuked, but she doubtless hated me anyway, as people usually do when they have injured someone undeservedly. It seems to be easier for us to forgive those who wrong us than those whom we have wronged.

The only other occasion on which I had to complain about a reporter was in the very early days, when there was no one to answer the telephone except myself and my secretary. I emerged from the study into the outer vestry on completion of an interview, and, having said goodbye to the client, listened to my secretary putting all her heart and soul into trying to help the person on the other end of the telephone. Suddenly, she seemed to freeze, went pale as death, put down the telephone and burst into tears. It turned out that the caller was a reporter on a local paper south of the river, who had had the bright idea of ringing up and pretending to be a client, to see what we would say. She told me that as soon as he mentioned that he was a reporter, she felt violated. That was the only hoax we had in the early days.

We are sometimes asked whether we get many hoaxes. The answer is "no". Anyone who rings up an organization like The Samaritans as a lark has probably some need of our services of which he or she is unconscious. It is not the kind of merry jape in which a normal person would engage, even if drunk. It is our policy to take every call seriously, and some which sound as though they are not very serious at the beginning turn out on examination to be from people who really do need help, but were not quite sure whether they were willing to ask for it, of us. I remember one evening I was knocking off for lunch at about 7.00 p.m., and passing through the outer vestry in an understandable hurry, overhearing a new young volunteer answering the emergency telephone and noticing that she was looking pink about the gills. She covered the mouthpiece and said it was a hoax and asked if she should hang up. I told her we did not get hoaxes, and to give the telephone to me. She hesitated, saying that I would not like to listen to the young man, who was speaking Anglo-Saxon. I took the phone firmly from her, and answered the young man patiently, and eventually a girl's voice replaced his. It appeared that she was pregnant by him and they neither of them wished to be married, so he had been trying to persuade her to have an abortion, and she had said she would if she could discuss it first with somebody in whom she could have confidence. She suggested The Samaritans, and he alleged that we were a lot of maiden aunts, and she said she did not think so, and he said, "I'll prove it"—and he nearly did. They both agreed to come round and discuss the matter, and both the marriage and the abortion were averted. The girl was looked after while she had her baby, which was subsequently adopted. Some hoax. Shortly afterwards we had a deputation from our colleagues in Miami, Florida, asking for advice on how to decrease the proportion of hoax calls. My reply was, "improve the quality of your answering, and you will find they are not hoaxes"; and I illustrated with the incident I have just described.

59

Nobody should join The Samaritans who is going to be put off by four-letter words or other forms of verbal aggressiveness or ribaldry. It is understandable if unprotected young girls, plagued by obscene telephone calls to their flats, appeal to the police to try to catch the person, but it is entirely different when such calls are made to The Samaritans. Women living alone or without a man about the house are liable to think that the caller is a huge caveman who will follow up his call by coming round and raping them, but volunteers in The Samaritans have no excuse for panicking, since they have learnt in the preparation classes that such characters are nearly always frightened little chaps who dare not even say, "Nice weather we've been having" to a girl if they met one face to face. These are pitiable people, who need help, and a Samaritan volunteer tries to persuade them of this, and convince them that they will not be walking into any trap if they come round to discuss their sexual difficulties with us. What appears in one's own home to be a horrid intrusion takes on a very different complexion when one is on duty in the office of an organization which exists to help people in every kind of difficulty arising out of poor human relationships. Those men who *do*, after receiving the same sort of answer from several different people, pluck up courage to come round and talk about their problem, are usually so easy to help that it is a pity so many of them just cannot believe that the whole thing is not a trick to get them arrested or beaten up.

Sexual problems (including marital problems, which nearly always have a sexual basis), account for three out of every eight of the more serious cases, and are only outnumbered by the psychological problems, many of them of course with some sexual content, which account for four out of eight—though only one of these four is psychiatric, i.e. requiring medical treatment as distinct from psychotherapy or psychological counselling. Of the sexual problems other than marital, the commonest is male homosexuality, which of itself causes very great distress in many cases, and, because of our existing laws, is an even more desperate condition than it would be if our laws were more enlightened. Amongst young people, there are worries about masturbation, unwanted pregnancy and fear of V.D., and amongst the middle-aged there are problems of impotence, alleged frigidity, and all kinds of frustration. People with sexual problems tend to feel excessively guilty, and often regard themselves as being beyond the pale, so that they require particularly gentle handling. The attitude of acceptance which Samaritan volunteers are taught to show to all clients is particularly important in the case of those with sexual problems, which clients may be ashamed to speak of at all unless the person they encounter inspires confidence, and is neither pruriently curious nor condemnatory.

Particularly in the larger cities, Samaritans have to be prepared to listen sympathetically and without being shocked to clients suffering from every deviation of aim or object in the textbooks, of some of which the volunteer may barely have heard. Fetishism, sado-masochism, voyeurism, exhibitionism, lesbianism, rape, incest, animality, transvestism, change of sex, male and female prostitution, are all things which may lead a human

61

being into a state where he or she just has to talk to someone who will not turn away in horror or stupidly suppose that the client must be having a wonderful time. All these things appear very different to one who is faced by a worried, shame-ridden fellow human being from what they seem when hinted at in the more sensational Sunday newspapers. People who like normal sex are the fortunate ones rather than the virtuous ones.

Psychological problems fall into three main groups: psychotic, psychoneurotic and psychopathic. No one seems to know what to do about the grossly psychopathic, but most of the psychoses and neuroses have an appropriate form of treatment, whether by physical means or by psychotherapy or a combination of both. People suffering from a psychotic illness are not normally amenable to psychotherapy, but medical treatments are often effective. The main forms of these illnesses are the schizophrenias, the paranoid states, and the manic-depressive illnesses, including endogenous depression. All these need medical treatment, and nothing else will do. The Samaritans are often successful in persuading sufferers from these illnesses to undergo treatment, and the one which most frequently leads to suicide, namely depressive illness, is the one which fortunately seems to respond best. Samaritan befriending may be helpful in the case of many psychotic illnesses. The various neuroses, such as anxiety states, may be so severe as to require medical treatment, or may respond to psychotherapy or psychological counselling, by someone who may or may not be a doctor. Probably all of us are to *some* extent neurotic, in the sense that we make use of various defences and pretexts and escapes in trying to cope with the world. The neurotic, unlike the psychotic, has not retreated into a world of illusion but is still living in the same world as the rest of us, though finding life difficult in various ways. Befriending has a very great part to play in helping those suffering from neuroses, especially the less severe ones which have to be lived with.

The Samaritans enjoy very good relations with the medical profession, largely because doctors know that they make no attempt to trespass on medical fields, and that they encourage clients to have a high regard for medicine in general and their own doctor in particular. On the rare occasions when the client's own doctor does not appear to be interested or to take seriously the client's desire for psychiatric attention, a way round is found without any criticism being made or implied about the doctor concerned. If a client changes his doctor, this is his own idea, not something suggested by The Samaritans. Every effort is made to persuade clients who seem to require psychiatry to allow their own doctor to arrange it, and only if they flatly refuse to permit their doctor to be approached (or if they do not have one in the same town) is a direct appointment sought for them. In the very large cities, there are more of such cases than in smaller towns, and also easier access to psychiatry via Casualty or Out-Patient Clinics. The vast majority of doctors are more concerned with the welfare of human beings than with the letter of their rights, and we have hardly ever had complaints arising out of the rare situations where a doctor did not know that a patient had seen a psychiatrist until the psychiatrist (who is not bound by the client's wishes as we are) notified him of this.

The Samaritans not only enjoy the co-operation of many doctors and the tolerance of most, but increasingly have patients recommended to them by both general practitioners and psychiatrists for the befriending which the doctor knows they urgently need. An American psychiatrist has stated that when prescribing for a patient he often wished to include TLC, which is not in the pharmacopoeia, but stands for 'tender loving care'. Most of us have this from our families and friends, but for those who possess neither, it is difficult to come by except in hospital. This is why so large a proportion of our mental hospital beds are occupied by patients who no longer need any treatment but who, if discharged, would soon be driven back by the same circumstances that brought them there in the first place.

Every Samaritan Branch has at least one Medical Consultant, usually a psychiatrist, to advise the Director or other Leaders, and in some cases actually to see clients whose problem appears to be a medical one.

Many clients are emotionally disturbed rather than mentally ill. They are not suffering primarily from some diagnosable and treatable mental condition, but are upset or agitated or depressed or confused because of some untoward circumstance or set of circumstances which they can no longer cope with alone. In these cases, though counselling may be of value, the most important thing is Samaritan befriending of the highest quality available. It is a great comfort in times of emotional distress to have a sympathetic person who will simply be with you and metaphorically hold your hand and refrain from giving you advice or telling you to pull yourself together when your problem is that you cannot pull yourself together. In some cases it is possible to give practical help in modifying the circumstances which have caused the distress, for instance by being instrumental in effecting a reconciliation between two people who have quarrelled, or suffered from some mis-understanding; or in sorting out problems relating to the person's work. Without attempting to engage amateurishly in casework, the volunteer can often, either directly or through the leadership, arrange for some at least of the client's worries to be removed.

One thing the experienced Samaritan volunteer will never do is to make light of something which is obviously causing the client great concern. People do often worry themselves sick about something which may appear to another person to be comparatively trivial, but if the volunteer regards it as trivial when told about it, it means that he is failing to put himself in the other person's place and look at things from his point of view. A Samaritan does not normally say such things as, "If I were you, I would do so-and-so," but if it *should* be right to say this, he would *mean*, "If I were you", and not, "If you were me". The Samaritan in the parable went where the injured man was, and the Samaritan volunteer has to go where the client is and be with him there, and not beckon him over to come where the Samaritan is.

One of the most difficult things for most of us to learn is how to bear the griefs and distresses of others, and to go on bearing them with them and for them until the whole load has been unburdened. The temptation is to intervene every time the client pauses for breath or to collect his thoughts, with some words of 'reassurance'. I have put the word in inverted commas because it is not the client who is being reassured, but the person who ought to be sharing his burdens and instead is throwing each one back, saying that it is not as heavy as is being suggested. All this "count your blessings, it's not as bad as you think" stuff is merely adding insult to injury. You insult a fellow human being by telling him that the things which have brought him almost to the verge of suicide are not as bad as all that. A real Samaritan is prepared to listen, and go on listening, and refrain from interrupting, and keep his bright suggestions until the end, when they will probably be seen to be unnecessary or irrelevant anyway, and be willing to bear and share the pain of it all with the sufferer without complaining that it is too much. Quite often, the mere fact of having been heard out, of somebody having listened and gone on listening until the whole story has been told, of being with somebody who cared enough to let it all become part of himself or herself, is all that is needed. The client goes away without having received any advice whatever but with more faith and hope and courage than he had when he came. This is the purest kind of Samaritan work, bearing and forbearing and sympathizing in the literal sense of 'suffering with' a fellow human being. The client thought nobody cared, or at least that nobody cared enough, but he has found someone who does care, enough to make the attempt to go on living worth-while. The theme song of many such clients could be, in the words of *Songs of Couch and Consultation*, "It's not that I haven't been loved, I haven't been loved *enough* to make me feel most properly loved."

In any Branch which is seriously getting to grips with its job, the proportion of spiritual problems will be low, because although many people have spiritual problems, these do not as frequently lead to the temptation to suicide as do psychological and sexual problems and problems of loneliness. Churchgoers form only about ten per cent of the population, and among the clients of The Samaritans the proportion is less than a quarter of this. It looks as though religious faith is, as one might expect, something which, where it exists, gives meaning and purpose to life and is therefore a protection against the desire to commit suicide; but it is not something which can be given *ad hoc* like a dose of medicine. Since the object of The Samaritans is the prevention of suicide, the organization is primarily concerned with those problems which most predispose to suicide, and any conscious spiritual need is usually a very minor part of the troubles that bring people to The Samaritans. The religious members of the organization do not preach religion to the clients, and the non-religious members do not preach against religion to the clients. If a client firmly and explicitly *asks* for religious instruction, this is arranged, and the agnostic members would be as assiduous in arranging this as a teetotal member would be in standing a client a drink (unless the client was an alcoholic in the one case or a religious maniac in the other).

67

Leaning over backwards to avoid inflicting personal beliefs on the client sometimes leads to the most unexpected people asking for some kind of spiritual help, which they would not have done if the Samaritan's attitude of trying to help the client to find what he himself wanted to be and believe had not inspired confidence in the Samaritan's integrity and unwillingness to exploit the client's vulnerable state of mind. The only preaching the Samaritans are allowed to do is in deeds, and if these do not themselves speak of love (which is the only unmistakable way to speak of God), then they will not convey this message more clearly by verbal puffs.

On one occasion in the early days (and my only excuse is that I was very tired) I slipped up on this, and told a client that God loved him. This was a silly thing to say, because although it was true, it could not possibly have appeared to the client to be true. Even allowing for exaggeration, he had had a dreadful life, and had every reason to suppose that if there were a god at all, this god had it in for him. He made a great show of staring into every corner of the room, and then said, "I do not see this person of whom you speak. My senses tell me that you are the only person here with me. Do *you* love me?" I shall always be grateful to that client for reminding me that even those of us who realize that most of God's loving of people is done through other people, and have consistently taught this, may ourselves slip up if we are not constantly on the watch against blah. Of course, there are sometimes circumstances in which the client *wants* to be told of God's love, but these are few and far between; almost always it is *our* love the client must be assured of, and that not merely by stating that it is so if our whole attitude contradicts this.

When I say that we must preach only by deeds, I do not mean that it is always necessary to *do* something. I have already indicated that there are instances where simply listening and caring are what the client most wants. Rushing round in small circles in a vain attempt to give such clients 'practical' help would be to fail them. True love expresses itself by being attentive to the client in order to discover what it is that he needs from us that we can rightly give. Perhaps the easiest clients to help are those for whom we are able to *do* something, however much trouble it may be, whose beneficial results we can plainly see. It may be that the deepest and most effective help we give is when we cannot think of anything to do, and feel, after the client has gone, that we were not able to help him at all: but we have borne it all with him, and feel like a piece of chewed string, and if "power has gone out" of us, the chances are it has gone into him.

Those of us who pray at all, pray for the clients with whom we have dealings, but we never pray *with* them except at their request. With some clients, one senses that they would be disappointed if one did not say "God bless you" or perhaps just "Bless you" on parting from them, and once that relationship has been established with a client so that you know the kind of person you are dealing with, it may be possible to tell him that he is remembered in your prayers. Sometimes he is pleased by this because he thinks there may, after all, be something in prayer, and sometimes he is pleased because it makes him feel as though he were almost a member of your family.

Of the clients who do want some kind of specifically religious comfort, the majority wish to make a confession and receive absolution, whether formally in church or informally in the room in which they are being interviewed. For those who believe in God, confession and absolution is a most potent means of help and healing. Rightly used, and applied to theological and not to pathological guilt, the confessional can give great peace of mind and renewed hope. Wrongly used, it can increase people's feelings of guilt and unworthiness, and it is sad to find how often this has been the effect of previous confessions made by some penitents who come to Samaritan priests. Where a penitent has been taught to regard as his major sins things which are either minor or not sins at all, the confessor has to begin by revising the confession and putting things in their correct order. He also has to impress upon the penitent that there are no limits to God's patience and forgiveness. Most important of all, absolution must be absolute: "Whosoever sins thou dost forgive, they *are* forgiven."

Some clients have been able to be helped effectively in the confessional where psychological methods of help have completely failed, but of course the converse is true, and there are some whose feelings of guilt can only be dealt with by competent psychotherapy. Befriending seems to help in a supplementary way in such cases by providing the acceptance of an 'ordinary' fellow human as well as the acceptance of a professional, which the client may feel is part of his professional equipment.

The same is true of clients who are being counselled about the more recondite sexual perversions: the acceptance of them by the person doing the counselling is sometimes discounted to some extent on the ground that those who are dealing with such matters every day become inured to them and would not turn a hair at anything, but if they find themselves being befriended by somebody who possibly finds such aberrations utterly incomprehensible and alien, and yet accepts them as part of the struggle of human beings who are coping, as all of us must, with our sexual needs as best we can, they cease to think of themselves as being beyond the pale.

Nobody could possibly envy those who are caught up in some compulsive activity, whether it be a sexual perversion or a drug addiction or a tedious obsessional ritual. Anyone who is under a compulsion to do things which mostly bring him little or no satisfaction is to be pitied, and deliverance from such compulsions is clearly not a matter of the person being confined in some moral strait-jacket, but a longed for liberation. The approach of those who consider that other people's 'misbehaviour' is invariably a deliberate and conscious choice of forbidden delights is not only stupid and false, but has no chance whatever of being helpful to the person concerned. It also indicates unrecognized difficulties in the person who is adopting this attitude. We all of us have a tendency, which needs to be watched, to do two opposite things in relation to other people's behaviour, and particularly sexual behaviour: namely, "compound for sins we are inclined to by damning those we have no mind to" and also "compound for sins we are inclined to by damning those we have a mind to." For instance, some of the most vicious letters written to newspapers about the Wolfenden report on homosexuality when analysed carefully gave every indication of having been written by latent homosexuals, though others were equally clearly written by people who had been fortunate in their transition at puberty to heterosexuality and who were completely lacking in the imaginative sympathy which permits one to understand difficulties one does not oneself experience.

Any Samaritan volunteer worthy of his membership soon learns the importance of Christ's command, "Judge not, that ye be not judged; condemn not, that ye be not condemned; for with what measure ye mete, it shall be measured to you again." Judging and condemning are such natural activities, so enjoyable to the natural man, that the Christian must regard the abandonment of them as a sign of supernatural power working in the person concerned, whether he would himself describe it in this way or not. Refraining from judging is not condonation, is not indifferentism, is not calling good evil and evil good; it is simply accepting one's status as a fellow human being of all other human beings, who are not to judge one another but are equally living under judgment.

One of the great problems is people who insist on judging *themselves*. They are often charitable towards other people, but towards themselves they are harsh. It is difficult to get them to realize that what appears to themselves to be setting a very high standard, if not a council of perfection, is in fact a great blasphemy arising out of deep spiritual pride.

Pride, and a sense of utter unworthiness, might appear to be complete opposites, and of course they sometimes are, but they are more closely connected than most of us care to admit unless we have considerable self-awareness and honesty. Relationships are therapeutic in so far as they encourage and increase these qualities. It is because the psychopathic and psychotic are not capable of insight that they are not amenable to psychotherapy, and because the neurotic find it so painful that skill and a strong personality, loving and unsqueamish, are required for it. The type of person who makes an effective Samaritan is similar. But so surgical an expression of this personality, essential for counselling, would be inappropriate for befriending, even if the befriender had the necessary knowledge. Psychotherapy, counselling and befriending are different functions, but the people who perform them in The Samaritans are all in their distinct ways Samaritan types, and they understand and value one another. For instance, psychiatrists who work closely with The Samaritans are themselves people who would be Samaritans if their professional function and duty did not disqualify them. It would be improper for people capable of giving medical treatment to employ their time and energies in befriending, which the lay person of similar calibre does at least equally well, and more acceptably to most clients because of the greater likelihood of common interests, and does so without danger of lapsing into professional detachment.

A Branch of The Samaritans ideally consists of people who are all truly Samaritans but whose function depends on other qualifications, so that doctors, theo-

logians, social workers, lawyers, etc. find themselves
acting as Consultants, either advising the Leadership
about clients, or seeing clients referred to them, or
both; parsons find themselves acting as Leaders,
directing the activities of the volunteers and sharing in
the work of counselling as far as they are able; whilst
lay people only are accepted as volunteers to do the
main work of befriending and interviewing. The cross-
fertilization between these three groups is of advantage
to all of them, and, most important, to the clients.

The way in which a new Branch is set up is now
prescribed by the Association on the basis of years of
experience in different places, and a brochure has been
issued for the guidance of those concerned. The
initiative has in the past come either from a doctor or
clergyman or other influential person, or from a body
such as a Clergy and Ministers' Fraternal, Council of
Christian Congregations, or in one or two cases from
Toc H or Rotary; where an enthusiastic enquirer is
not in a position of influence, he is invited to try to
interest someone who is. In due course a Steering
Committee is formed, which arranges either an Invitation Meeting to which the sort of people who might
become Leaders or Consultants are invited, or a Public
Meeting which anyone, as well as these, may attend;
or both. Once the decision is made to try to establish a
Branch in the area, and a Committee, with a Convenor,
is elected, the Council of Management may recognize
this Committee and those associated with it as a Preparatory Group. This Group is entitled to use the name
of The Samaritans in its publicity, and it has the task

of finding an Acting Director (who must be approved by the Association) and other Leaders, Consultants (this is the easiest task) and, above all, volunteers, for whom a course of Preparation Classes is arranged by the Association. The Committee meanwhile seeks suitable premises, obtains an easily-memorized telephone number, and raises the necessary funds. As soon as all this has been done and a sufficient number of volunteers selected and instructed, a date is fixed for the service to come into operation by the emergency number being advertised, and the Preparatory Group, with the approval of the Association, becomes a Probationary Branch as from this date. Branches remain Probationary, with non-voting observers instead of voting representatives on the Council of Management of the Association, for at least a year, and the Director remains an Acting Director until he has attended an annual School for Directors, or one of the annual Conferences, or some equivalent occasion which allows the Association to satisfy itself that he knows his job and is himself a 'Samaritan type'. The Executive Committee of the Council of Management, which has an Extension Sub-Committee, arranges for every Branch to be Visited annually by two of a panel of visitors, to maintain communication between the Branches and the Executive and to encourage the members in their work, as well as to ensure that the principles and methods of the Association are working well in that Branch. The Council of Management interferes as little as possible with the Branches, because in emergency work the people on the spot must make their own decisions. It tries only to ensure that centres using the Samaritan name should be recognizably the same everywhere, inspired by the same spirit, and differing only as local circumstances require; and it preserves the Samaritan ethos not by detailed regulations and directives, but by retaining the appointment of the Director (or Chairman) of each Branch in its own hands, on the recommendation of the Branch Committee. Directors are appointed or re-appointed each year, and this is not automatic: the Association has a plain duty to appoint the person who will help the clients most by making the Branch as truly 'Samaritan' as it can be.

The whole organization is client-centred. The clients are its sole *raison d'être*: it has no other object, main or subsidiary, than to serve the clients in such a way that they will stay alive and be glad to be alive and be enabled to live "more abundantly". Every detail of the methods and principles of The Samaritans has been worked out in the light of clients' actual needs as dis-covered by experience, and instructions about ways of working are normally conveyed to those concerned in the words "The needs of the clients dictate that . . ." The Director of a Branch may appear to be a dictator, and his authority is unquestioned in a Samaritan Branch, because "the needs of the clients dictate that decisions should be swiftly made and loyally executed without dithering, for 'in the multitude of counsellors there is confusion' ". But standing over every Director is *his* dictator, an amalgamation of the clients with whom he has had to deal and from whom he has learnt by patient and imaginative observation what clients need.

Clients contemplating suicide need to be able to get in touch at any time with a minimum of effort: hence the emergency telephone. They need to be able to 'test the temperature' before committing themselves: hence the possibility of remaining anonymous at the beginning of the conversation, or indefinitely, if they wish. They need to retain their freedom of action, and to remain in control of their own destinies whilst still having some sort of help: hence the confidentiality, and the assurance that nothing whatever will be done against their will—no one will pick them up in a plain van and lock them up in a padded cell, or even call and see them without their permission. They need a friend to turn to, who will simply be that and nothing more unless and until they express a wish for something more from someone in the organization: hence the provision that the telephone is answered in the first instance by a volunteer—not a doctor, for they have rung because they do not want to ring a doctor, and not a parson or social worker, for the same reason. They need someone who can get them more expert help if this is required: hence the structure of the organization, and the other, non-emergency telephone with another member to use it. They may need someone to go to them who cannot leave the telephone: hence the 'Flying Squad'. They may need to speak to someone of a different sex or age or kind from the one who first answered: hence the mixture of volunteers on duty. They may need to talk to someone more expert at once, perhaps in the middle of the night: hence 'Home Service'. They may need to ring several times till they hear a voice that inspires confidence: hence the duty roster with its constant changes, and the refusal to log heavy breathing or incoherent sobs as a hoax. They need above all to know that they have *nothing to lose*, and perhaps everything to gain, by ringing The Samaritans: hence the care with which the volunteers are chosen, deployed, instructed and supervised.

In a word, they need love.

How love is to express itself is a matter on which not all who 'feel a concern' for the potentially suicidal are agreed. There are some who are convinced that only medically qualified people ought to encounter the potential suicide in an emergency situation, because of the high proportion of cases of mental illness and the inability of unqualified people to make diagnoses. The Samaritans can only welcome the establishment of medical emergency centres for the suicidal, for the people who approach these are by hypothesis willing to recognize their need of a doctor; but they do not believe that such a centre can make The Samaritans unnecessary, for it is a fact of experience that many suicidal persons will not entertain the idea of psychiatry, and also that some who may accept psychiatry have other needs which a doctor cannot supply but which The Samaritans sometimes can.

The chief *medical* centres for the prevention of suicide are the Suicide Research Centre in Los Angeles, U.S.A., under Dr. Shneidman and Dr. Farberow, and *Lebensmüdefürsorge* (Care for those who are weary of life) in Vienna, under Dr. Erwin Ringel. The former does not use lay volunteers; the latter makes some use of the members of 'Caritas', a Roman Catholic lay organization. Three European Conferences have been led by

Dr. Ringel: Vienna, 1960, at which the Samaritans were represented by Mrs. Nuran Ulupinar, Director of our Istanbul Branch, and myself; Copenhagen, 1963, at which the Samaritans were represented by Professor Erwin Stengel, one of the Presidents of our Association, and author of *Suicide and Attempted Suicide*[1] (required reading for Samaritan Leaders); and Basle, 1965.

At the other extreme, there are those who are convinced that the potential suicide who seeks non-medical help is to be regarded as a person with a spiritual problem, whether he recognizes this or not, and that the object of emergency aid by telephone should be to lead him to acceptance of the Christian Faith in the form in which this is held by the Church or group of Churches responsible for the service. The Samaritans have many objections to this. First, it does not get to grips with the problem of suicide, for it is just not true that any large proportion of potential suicides can be deterred by evangelization, and if some suicidal people are helped, it will be because of the attention they receive from persons who in many cases are kindly as well as pious, rather than because of the preaching of the Gospel in words. Secondly, it leaves out of account not only those who may need psychiatric help but also members of non-Christian faiths, members of Churches with which the Church or group of Churches offering the service have little in common, and the even larger category of those who, though nominally Christians, distrust the Church for the very reason that they suspect that its representatives *will* seek to serve its own interests rather than serve the client disinterestedly.

[1] Pelican, 1964.

Thirdly, it leads to the scandal of rival services, Roman Catholic and Protestant, in the same city. Fourthly, it tends to become clerical (in Sweden, for instance, it is always a priest who answers the telephone). Fifthly, though it may attract some volunteers who have a 'Samaritan' spirit, it must attract others whose main objective is the making of converts. Sixthly, some of those whose offer to help could hardly be declined by such a service, because of their impeccable religious qualifications, would be rejected by The Samaritans on the ground that their approach would tend to make some clients feel even more guilty and more unworthy, and thus increase the risk of suicide.

Naturally, any group of people has the right to organize a centre which the general public is invited to telephone, for any purpose the law allows. Such a group can direct its invitation specially to the suicidal if it wishes, provided it does not use the name 'The Samaritans' or 'The Telephone Samaritans', which are registered by our Association. (The many other societies which incorporate the word 'Samaritan' are not concerned with the prevention of suicide by emergency telephone.) An openly evangelistic service such as 'Telephone Ministry' is not likely to be confused with The Samaritans, and the criticisms I have made apply only to services which in certain continental towns claim to be roughly equivalent to The Samaritans.

My idea of an emergency service for potential suicides received widespread publicity not only in the United Kingdom but also on the Continent and in other parts of the world. As early as the spring of 1954 a man who had read about me in a Greek newspaper hitch-hiked all the way from Salonika to see me; another man wrote from Havana, Cuba, about a very recondite sexual problem; and a man telephoned me in heavily-accented English from Copenhagen saying he could only afford three minutes and how could he prevent a girl in his office from committing suicide? (I said: "I don't need three minutes, just three words: stay with her." He thanked me, and then asked "But what if she wants to go to the toilet?" I told him: "This is no time for prudery: don't let her lock herself in *anywhere*. As long as you stay with her, she's safe, and you'll find out what else you need to do." I never heard what happened, but I am used to that.) It was not many months later that a Roman Catholic priest wrote from Kyoto, the ancient capital of Japan, to ask me about the prevention of suicide, since many Japanese travelled specially to Kyoto to commit suicide there.

An article in a Swiss paper described my work and also that of a Free Church Minister who for some months in 1954 advertised an Ilford telephone number for suicidal people to ring but then emigrated to the United States. The paper confused the two of us and attached his name to a photograph of me and some of my earliest volunteers, but this did not matter, since the idea was publicized in German and attracted the attention of pastors who later started anti-suicide work in Hälsingborg, Sweden, West Berlin and Zürich, except that the emphasis in these places at that time was on the ministry of an individual pastor—something I had already abandoned.

Although by 1954 The Samaritans was no longer a one-man band, I was kept too busy to make any attempt to organize similar services in other places, even in Great Britain, so it is not surprising that the centres which began operations a couple of years later on the Continent differed considerably from my original model, even though in some cases the organizers did not rely only on magazine articles for their information but also wrote to me for advice. To some extent, differences of method of working arise out of national differences, but these may easily be exaggerated: human beings are much the same everywhere, and most differences that still exist seem to me to arise from a different conception from that of disinterested 'Samaritan' help for clients irrespective of their race or creed.

No Continental service adopted the name 'Samaritans', and this is a good thing, not only because few of these services were akin to The Samaritans in their structure, principles and methods, but also because the name does not evoke the same image as in the English-speaking world. When our Branch in Istanbul started, we readily agreed that the appropriate name for it was the Turkish for 'Comrades in the Spirit' or 'Spiritual Sputniks' (*Canyoldaşlari Cemiyeti*), and when a Branch was formed in Tel Aviv, Israel (which unfortunately lasted only a few months) it was unthinkable that it should be called 'The Samaritans', so it was named '*Yad v'Ezer*' (Helping Hand). This is similar to the name adopted by the Swiss services: '*Die Dargebotene Hand*'—'*La Main Tendüe*'—'The Proffered Hand'. The French chose the lovely name '*L'Amitié*' (Friendship) in Paris, and on the Riviera, where this might be misinterpreted to mean 'Call-Girls', '*S.O.S. par Téléphone*'. The Low Countries also stressed the telephone, with '*Télé-*

Acceuil' (Tele-Welcome) in Belgium and '*Telefonische-Hulpdienst'* (Telephone Help Service) in the Netherlands; and Germany added an ecclesiastical flavour to this with its '*Telefonseelsorge*' (Pastoral Care by Telephone). In the United States, Fr. K. Murphy of Boston, Massachusetts, after correspondence with me, launched 'Rescue, Inc.', and Miami, Florida had the brilliant idea of inviting people to dial the letters F-R-I-E-N-D-S. (If ever we have a Branch in Ruislip, I hope the owner of RUI 2433 will make us a present of it, as it is what you would get if you dialled S-U-I-C-I-D-E. The number corresponding to 'Friends' does not exist on the London system.)

It was not until 1959 that the second centre called 'Telephone Samaritans' was founded: this was appropriately in the northern capital, Edinburgh, on the initiative of the Rev. (now Prof.) James Blackie. The first centre in England outside London was started at Liverpool in 1960 by the then Rector, the Rev. Christopher Pepys, now Bishop of Buckingham. Our first and only centre in Northern Ireland was established in Belfast in 1961, and it was a great triumph for the Samaritan ideal that in a city where religious conflicts were often so violent, the Director, the Rev. W. G. M. Thomson, a Presbyterian, was assisted from the beginning by an Anglican, a Roman Catholic and a Methodist. The three men named in this paragraph are all members of the Executive of the Association, together with the Rev. Basil Higginson (Manchester), the Rev. John Eldrid (Portsmouth—formerly my assistant in London), Mr. David Arthur (Aberdeen), Mr. Arthur Frymann (Nottingham), Mr. Nadir Dinshaw (Bombay), and our two Consultant Psychiatrists, Dr. Doris Odlum and Dr. Richard Fox.

Although I gave what help I could in the founding of new centres, both by correspondence and by paying visits when invited to do so, the demands of the work in London were too great for me to feel any temptation to try to set up actual *branches* of The Samaritans of St. Stephen Walbrook, integrated with us and coming, however flexibly, under my supervision. Indeed, I had my hands so full that I think I should have been unable to carry on had not the Gulbenkian Foundation come to the rescue in 1959 with a most generous grant, which continued for six years, to enable me to have the help of a paid staff (which only the biggest cities require). It was hoped that I should be set free sufficiently to organize more and more centres, but a variant of Parkinson's Law increased the number of London clients to take up all the time of my staff *and* myself. It was not until 1963 that it became imperative to form an Association without any further delay, and the twenty-one centres in existence at that time banded together as Foundation Members of a Company Limited by Guarantee, licensed by the Board of Trade to omit the word 'Limited' from its title.

The founding Branches were Aberdeen, Belfast, Bombay, Bournemouth, Brighton, Cambridge, Dundee, Edinburgh, Glasgow, Hong Kong, Hull, Jersey, Karachi, Liverpool, London, Manchester, Portsmouth, Reading, Salisbury (Rhodesia), Stoke-on-Trent and Woolwich. There were at that time in addition sixteen Probationary Branches and fifteen Preparatory Groups.

They differed considerably from one another in

their traditions; but thanks to the Samaritan spirit they were able to weld themselves into a harmonious organization within eighteen months, and the rapid spread of the movement and the improvements in our practice which have taken place since the Association was formed are the proof that this was a right, and probably overdue, step. The strength of the Association lies in its Branches, one of which is the original London centre; and it has no headquarters: it is admirably served by its full-time Secretary, Mrs. Daphne Morriss, working from her flat at Beckenham, and the Hon. Bursar, Mr. Leslie Kentish. The Council of Management meets twice a year, always in a different town: it comprises one representative from each full Branch. Its Executive Committee meets every two months, and between meetings I, as Chairman, have to make its day to day decisions. Never a day goes by without some query or request for help from some Branch.

The formation of the Association was prepared for by National Conferences. We call them this, although with Branches in Turkey, Rhodesia, India, Pakistan, Hong Kong and New Zealand we are international, because there are International Conferences every two years of the *Centre International d'Information des Services de Secours par Téléphone*, which was set up at Promenade St. Antoine, Geneva, with Pasteur Reynald Martin as Secretary, as a result of the International Congress held at Château de Bossey, near Geneva, in September 1960 on the initiative of M. Georges Lillaz, President of the French movement. This conference in fact preceded both the Vienna Conference of Dr. Ringel and our own first 'National' Conference, held at Balliol College,

Oxford, in 1961. In 1962 our Conference was at Durham
and the International one at Bad Boll, near Stuttgart,
and in 1963, at Sheffield, we had our first Conference
since the formation of the Association. In 1964, the
country in which the movement began played host to
the Third International Congress, at Christ Church,
Oxford, and at this we elected an International Committee with myself as President, Pfarrer Otto Kehr (who
had presided at the second Congress) of Germany,
Pfarrer Ernst Schwyn (who had presided at the first
Congress) of Switzerland, M. G. Lillaz of France,
Abbé Parée of Belgium, Ds. P. Noomen of Holland,
Komminister E. Frizell of Scandinavia, and the Secretary. That year we divided our own Conference into
Northern and Southern sections, at Dundee and
Oxford respectively, but in 1965 returned to the plan
of one Conference, at Manchester University. In 1966
there is to be an International Congress in Mexico City,
as the next in Europe is not to be until 1967, in Brussels.

The papers which make up the second half of this
book were all read at one or other of the conferences I
have mentioned; and two things are noteworthy about
them. First, that the lay volunteers, who greatly out-
number Leaders and Consultants at Samaritan Conferences, find it natural that most speakers should be
Samaritan psychiatrists, whose papers should be read
with the nature of the audience in mind; and secondly,
that the lectures demonstrate both the differences of
approach to the same subjects by the various lecturers,
and the underlying unity of attitude amongst those
closely associated with The Samaritans. Although The
Samaritans has been forced to become an organization,

in order to serve more clients better, it is more like an organism, living and growing and developing. It refuses to become ossified, seeks harmony rather than uniformity, and is prepared to scrap even the oldest tradition and jettison any method proved ineffective in serving the needs of the clients. Only one thing is sacrosanct, and that is the task to which, and the spirit in which, we have dedicated ourselves: namely, to behave like the Good Samaritan in the parable towards those who are tempted to suicide or despair.

Helping people in distress

Dr. H. J. Walton
Hon. Psychiatric Consultant to the Edinburgh Samaritans

A man I saw recently said to me that he was being helped very considerably by the "Good Samaritans". This slip or misunderstanding about the name of the organization exposed the man's expectations. He wanted to be helped while he remained the passive, helpless recipient of benefits resulting from the exertions of the good Samaritans.

There will be those of us who do not see our main exertion as consisting of a display of goodness. Nor will we think our job is to give material supplies to those calling upon our skills. In a bread-and-blanket situation, in which the helpless person is also a recipient of material benefits, it is clear that the danger we run is to foster dependency, imposing further weakening through taking too much upon ourselves.

Goodness itself need not be a prominent aspect of the transactions of those who help others. If we are good to people, that is pleasant both for them and for us; but we would be hard pressed to be objective in reckoning afterwards the success of the transaction if goodness were our criterion. Much more appropriately, we can use as our yardstick the notion of effectiveness. The question we will then ask after each intervention in the life of another person is: How effective was I in the dilemma with which I was presented?

To assess whether our intervention was effective

requires of us that we should specify what view we take of people in general, and to what aspect of a person we direct our exertions when we undertake to help.

Every person who consults us consists of four separate aspects: his physical body; his brain and its executive functions: his mind and its varying activities; and finally his social background and social relationships. A behaving individual is a person in whom these four systems of organization are acting simultaneously.

People like us, members of the professions or groups who aim to be helpful to people in distress may direct efforts at the body, attending to physical illness, discomfort or abnormality. Doctors have the responsibility to determine whether illness which can be corrected is affecting a disturbed person.

Secondly, there are now powerful drugs which can act on the brain, and armies of people try to reduce their distress by using large amounts of tranquillizers or sleeping pills. Thirdly, it may be at the mind which efforts are directed, and this is why psychiatry plays a central part in efforts to alleviate distress. It is, however, to the last aspect of personal organization that I will confine my remarks: a person's social background and social relationships as the source of his distress and also the area in which we can intervene to cure his distress.

In our attempt to understand people, their social situation and social relationships are of great significance. People need social relationships as much as they need food. Man always functions in a social setting. He is enabled as a child in the family group to learn the social expectations others have about him and the social skills he will require for normal living. When the person reaches maturity he has built into his personality the customs, the manners and the values of the society in which he was reared.

The child's social adequacy improves with each stage in his development; by school age he is ready to progress with growing independence through increasingly complicated social settings, after he has learned in the family about the demands society will make on him and the satisfaction it will permit him to enjoy.

A person in adulthood feels 'good' to the extent that his relations with his parents were satisfactory. A person who had bad relations with a parent will be prone, throughout life, to experience spells of 'bad' feelings: self-criticism, inferiority, depression or anxiety. In this sense the exact nature of a person's associations with his parents remain embedded in him and are a source of feeling states which can occur to him throughout adulthood.

The people we see in crisis, therefore, talk to us about their present social relationships, their own family members, and at length also about relationships they had with their parents.

A person communicates with other people by means of speech. He communicates with himself by thinking. Thought is internal behaviour. In an interview we enable the person we are helping to give us access to his internal behaviour, by asking him to tell us about his thoughts.

In our attempt to understand behaviour through talking to a person, a double task faces us. We have to understand the person in the first place, and then we have to comprehend the situation in which he finds himself. When his crisis is the result of external difficulties or pressures, we can talk of *press*, as when someone loses an important person through death. When the crisis is the result of internal pressures inside the troubled individual, we can speak of *stress*. Such internal stress can be produced by thoughts in a person's mind, by feelings such as anger or resentment, or by impulses such as sexual urges which trouble the person but which he cannot allow full expression.

A useful way of looking at people in crisis may be by assuming that when they contact us they are disturbed by painful inner tension: they suffer from anxiety which has reached an insupportable level. Anxiety is caused by the human environment. It is a mood of fear which puts out of action a whole range of normal skills and functions. An anxious person does not attend adequately to his environment, does not notice things, makes errors, is forgetful. Generally, anxiety serves to disorganize ordinary behaviour.

Anxiety can increase in intensity to produce a state of terror. If a person is appropriately predisposed, there is a wide range of life events which can precipitate a state of anxiety.

Being rejected by another person is one: as when an employee gets told that his work is not good enough, or a husband tells his wife that her housekeeping does not satisfy his expectations. (Perhaps his standards are overconscientiousness ingrained in him by an excessively perfectionist mother when he was young.)

The other person may precipitate anxiety in our client or patient by more clear-cut aggression or hostility, making threats which endanger the security of the person who consults us. It can be, however, that there is no other person prominently implicated; instead it may be a person's own thoughts which precipitate anxiety in him: a mother suffering from fearfulness that she is not good enough to care for her child and will inadvertently perpetrate some harmful or even fatal accident. Thoughts connected with sex are often extremely distressing to people, and if we get from them details about their past lives, it is clear how the conflict state about sex arose. They need to express their responses of loving and physical tenderness, but there are forbidding images or memories lodged in their mind which forbid such natural expressions of love.

We arrive at mature forms of sexuality only in adulthood, passing through phases which society considers abnormal, indeed will not recognize as customary or common at certain stages of life. We forget the devious paths by which adolescents arrive at mature sexuality.

A man of twenty-three whose parents were devout Seventh Day Adventists said: "When I was twelve, our teacher at school gave us a talk on masturbation. I remember feeling very guilty because I imagined he was talking just to me. He told us it was no disgrace to masturbate if it was indulged in occasionally, but it could be very detrimental if indulged in too often. He spoke about wearing oneself out and other things. I have always been slight and never was at all muscular. I formed the conclusion I was so thin because I masturbated. I was under the impression that the signs that I masturbated were written all over me, so I would never go to the sea or to a swimming pool for a swim. I was ashamed of my build. Now comes the point I fail to understand. During my first years at high school, I was homosexually inclined. The sight of a boy's erect penis used to send thrills of ecstasy through me. This may not sound good at all, but still, it is the truth. Then it left me, my homosexual feelings, but the habit of masturbation remained with me."

This young man went on to achieve an adequate sexual adaptation, only occasionally troubled by the thoughts of sexual guilt in his mind which could at times make him extremely anxious. There are people, however, who turn to us for help, who are not able to proceed at all in aspects of their personal growth. Their thoughts have spread out to lead to actual behaviour which cripples them. I can best illustrate this by using the words spoken by a woman when in an anxious state: "The greatest difficulty and the one terror of my life is the sexual difficulty. I always thought I would never marry. Even now I can't bear my husband to touch me. I love him deeply and he cares just as much for me, but I don't like him to come near me. I don't know how I can express the hatred I have of being touched by my husband. He says I am hopeless. He shouts at me: 'Why did you ever marry? You should have stayed without a husband!' I love my husband, but I hate ever to see his body."

This woman has had to exclude entirely the sexual side of her nature from her awareness. When her husband's sexual wishes obtrude, she is shaken out of her denial of sexuality and then experiences extreme misery. Her solution has been to banish such thoughts entirely. As long as she can avoid this feared area of living she can manage. When her marriage circumstances compel her to admit the facts of sexual living, she is helpless and desperate. This maldevelopment in her personality will never be put right. The time when it could have been relieved is already past.

The person who contacts us, we are considering, will usually be in a state of excessive anxiety. This is a painful inner state, a pervasive sensation of fear which is uncomfortable and in extreme cases may be intolerable. Anxiety is so distressing a state that, when it is severe, the sufferer will seek to reduce the painful tension, sometimes in ways which lead him to suffer great harm.

Those who see many anxious people are struck by the remarkable fact that there are various kinds of anxiety. The importance of distinguishing the type of anxiety lies in the fact that for each type a different kind of approach is required. I will mention the three main types of anxiety. A person may have extreme, massive anxiety because he fears he will be suddenly isolated, or because he suddenly is overwhelmed with self-reproach or self-loathing, or because he dreads some harm is about to befall him in relation to his body.

The first type of anxiety, the dread of isolation, occurs when a person is suddenly deprived of the support of another person, upon whom he had been more deeply dependent than perhaps he knew. He may lose the protecting person through death; a woman may lose the husband on whom she was emotionally dependent because he leaves her for another woman; a person may never have married in order to retain the protectiveness of a parent, and be precipitated into an anxiety attack if the parent withdraws affection or support.

This type of separation anxiety has been studied in small children who are taken from parents when admitted to hospital; but you can also see very similar reactions in adults, say in a woman whose husband leaves on a business trip overseas, or in someone whose more emotionally-robust marriage partner becomes ill.

11) Self disgust.

The second type of anxiety we encounter, the anxiety of self-disgust, is different. Healthy people have a reasonable appreciation of their own attainments; they tell themselves that, considering the obstacles they have encountered, they have acquitted themselves fairly adequately. But the anxiety which comes from an unhealthy conscience leads a person to think that he has failed, that he betrayed all the trust reposed in him, that he is a disgrace to those who had believed in him. This type of anxiety leads the person to say to whoever is approached for help: "Please don't let my mother or father hear of this." Such a person will figuratively beat his head, overcome with self-hatred and abnegation. They may say that they deserve only condemnation or punishment. Some may actually punish themselves, taking their chastisement in their own hands. You may know the passage from Donne: "Some have beat out their braines at the wal of their prison, and some have eate the fire out of their chimneys: and one is said to have come neerer our case than so, to have strangled himself, though his hands were bound, by crushing his throat between his knees."[1]

[1] John Donne, *Devotions*, XII.

These people are flayed by their consciences. Psychologically they have, as part of their minds, attitudes of self-disgust. These attitudes are seen by psychiatrists as stemming from hatred or criticism or rejection experienced during growing up. Disliked by a parent, they have come to carry for ever, as part of their mentality, the inner reflection of what was once directed upon them from the censorious parent. Now it has become a part of the self. Any criticism they evoke, a failure of their efforts, or even a reproof uttered by someone in the heat of anger, suddenly lights up their own stores of self-criticism. Only someone who has experienced the horror of being alone in a state of terror while the full light of consciousness plays relentlessly over all the weakness, failures, omissions and faults, can understand the fear which may be felt by somebody who regards himself as beyond contempt. Often such a person, when seeking help, is in an extreme dread that he has failed, that he is an outcast and will be despised if only people knew. Often such a person conveys the circumstances in which his self-disgust was acquired. One woman said: "My mother did not give me the love a daughter needs. I was aware of this throughout my life. I was a stranger to my mother which made me feel horrible. She had no notion of what I suffered." A man said: "The way my mother treated me! The way she's always treated me! I know that before my birth my mother went to several people to try and bring me down. I know how little she thought of me. I knew I wasn't wanted by my mother when I was a child. As soon as I got my senses, as long as I can remember, I knew that! She hated me."

We recognize that when a person seeks our help for

anxiety of this self-despising variety we will probably find in his life history a parent who was not able to feel appropriate affection for him. This parent is then retained in his mind throughout life, as a sort of inner assailant, who can undermine him, bring him down, humiliate him. His precarious self-esteem drops to an agitatingly low level when in addition he encounters criticism or rejection in his current experience with other people.

The third type of anxiety, dread of physical damage, may be illustrated by its expression in a young man: "Lately I go to bed many nights haunted by the fear that I won't wake up the following morning. I can assure you this fear of dying is torture to go through."

The person is suddenly struck with terrible certainty by a fear that his heart is diseased, or that he has a cancer. People anxious in this way, overcome by a fear of some serious physical affliction, are likely to seek medical reassurance directly, so they are more prone to have their first recourse to doctors than to any other sort of helping person.

To give first aid to people with these varying types of anxiety calls for very different responses in the helping person. The individual with separation anxiety needs substitute company from a friend or a relative, or hospital care. The person with conscience anxiety, convinced of his worthlessness, needs a personal response which will revive his self-esteem. To protect and provide comfort and care for him, as advocated for the earlier type of separation anxiety, may only convince him of his worthlessness. The person with the third type of anxiety, fear of bodily dissolution, usually needs medical

G

attention as a first step, before tracing out with him what the roots of his physical panic were.

While we may approve of the wisdom of those in trouble who seek help, they themselves may consider their help-seeking despicable. Jerome Frank[1] has demonstrated that one of the changes occurring in people who are successfully treated by psychiatrists is their greater effectiveness in getting help for themselves when they feel troubled. Some people approaching us will show, as part of their personality disturbance which has not yet been improved by treatment, a great hesitancy in asking for help. Many of our clients or patients will reach us only when the extremity of their distress has pushed them over this inner barrier against asking for aid. They will often be ashamed and apologetic at this weakness, as they see it, this lapse into open admission of lack of independence. Many will not come to see us until their distress has driven them to contemplate suicide.

Often we may see a person when he is already determined on taking an active step to deal with his distress, the step of self-injury. William James said that only very unimaginative people can never have contemplated suicide at some stage of their lives. Most people who die by suicide are solitary; they are more often men than women: they live on the fringe of society, without close or warm personal ties.[2] They are clearly unlike the general run of people, in that they are con-

---

[1] J. Frank, *Persuasion and Healing* (John Hopkins Press: Baltimore, 1961).

[2] P. Sainsbury, *Suicide in the London Boroughs* (O.U.P., 1954).

spicuously deprived of the interest and reassurance which comes from associating with loving people.

However, suicide is contemplated or even attempted by quite ordinary people, and they contact us for help either when they begin thinking about self-injury or after they have made an attack upon themselves with drugs or by cutting at a blood vessel.

A suicide attempt usually implies that the person behaving self-destructively is angry. The anger which was turned upon himself in the self-injury had been intended for another person: a woman intends to revenge herself upon the husband who neglected her, a parent reproaches the children who were not sufficiently obedient, a child by attempting suicide reproaches the parents who failed to understand.

The great importance, from our point of view, of suicidal inclinations is the need which the afflicted person has to talk. It is of the utmost importance that such a person should be given the chance to clear out of his thoughts the full circumstances of his anger, expressing in detail the conditions which led him to lay a hand to his life. A woman said: "My husband admitted his affair with that woman, and said he was not even ashamed of it. I had to go through having my baby and, in the meantime, they were corresponding with each other every day, and she was phoning him up at the office. I begged my husband to please see me through my confinement with consideration and not see the woman through the two weeks it would take me to have my baby. I begged him to give me a chance to love him. He looked at me with loathing in his eyes. I had my baby and dutifully he visited me every day, with his mind miles away. I said to my husband that I was definitely going to take my life. I said to him: 'I don't want to live any more. I am going to die.' He just laughed. So I took an overdose of sleeping pills."

For such a person to talk, and to have what she says listened to seriously, is to look afresh at the difficulties which had seemed insoluble. A suicide attempt is always an opportunity to explore and help the distressed person to give outward expression to latent reserves of anger, and then to plan a constructive alternative reaction to the frustrating person at whom the suicide attack pointed.

What is still more important is the opportunity provided when a person makes contact before a suicide attempt, an opportunity to prevent it. When we see a dejected person, and inquire directly, once we have established a relationship with him, whether any thought of suicide preoccupies him, we make it possible for the intention to be discussed. Once the intending suicide has spoken his thoughts aloud, the chances that he will go on to attempt suicide are greatly reduced.

Often the person in distress makes contact with the helping agency at the time of a personal disaster. The correct approach, of course, is to allow the person to talk in detail about his setback or injury or loss. To do so may be of crucial importance, in that, if the chance is not provided, feelings will become closed over and obscured. However, although subsequently disguised, they are not rendered ineffective. They continue to exert a harmful and even crippling effect on the person.

An illustration may be provided by the mourning

experience. Bereavement can be responded to in one of three ways.[1] The grief reaction can be immediate and intense: this is normal grief, which is followed by restlessness and moods of depression. A bereaved person normally sleeps poorly, may be troubled by vivid mental images of the dead person, who gradually is thought of less as other interests supervene.

The grief reaction can be abnormally prolonged, and the sorrowing person then appears as a case of depression. For as long as two years after the death he suffers from anxiety and is unable to detach himself from preoccupation with the dead person. Another common abnormality is a delayed grief reaction, the sorrow being experienced a long time after the death of the loved person; there had been no reaction when mourning was to be expected. Later on, some future minor loss may trigger off a disproportionately great depression.

The grief reaction may be entirely suppressed, not occurring at all; instead the bereaved person may subsequently develop symptoms of a physical type, like headaches, or, particularly in the case of younger people, a behaviour disorder like delinquency.

Only in recent years have we come to realize that bereaved people require to respond actively to their loss. Unless what has been called the "grief work" is performed, abnormal types of grief take place. These can probably be avoided if, as a first aid measure, the mourner is given proper help to express his sense of distress and loss.

[1] C. M. Parkes, "Grief as an Illness", *New Society*, 9th April 1964.

If we adopt the formula that people who contact us in crisis are those in whom anxiety has risen to unmanageable levels, we have still to ask ourselves what view we require to take of those few people who contact us, perhaps repeatedly, and in whom we can discern no evident anxiety. What do these un-anxious people want from us?

We may get further if we watch for masked anxiety, assuming that the person consulting us has found measures with which this painful feeling state can be neutralized to some extent. We then require to discover the devices which enabled the person to achieve this more comfortable state. What signs must we aim to observe in those people who consult us but do not show apparent anxiety?

There are numerous psychological reactions with which a person can prevent, reduce or terminate anxiety which troubles him. He can actually distort his sense of awareness, deny that what troubles him is present in reality at all.

A person can move away from difficulties, isolating himself, and in the process cut off vitally important ties with others. A man who is timid in his relationship towards a colleague may misguidedly give up his work in the mistaken view that this will solve the difficulty he had in the particular personal relationship. Adequate counselling would help such a man to respond more aggressively to his dominating colleague while staying in his job. Doing so may increase the feeling of anxiety; the helping person can permit him to share and express these painful sensations until he has mastered his troublesome personal relationship.

Some people have had to cope with painful levels of anxiety since early in life. They may have tried to control it by cures that prove to be worse than the tension itself. We may see them, then, not for the original anxiety, but now complaining of the cure they have attempted.

Alcoholism is a case in point: an attempted self-cure. The insecure man has need of alcohol to relieve his anxiety when in the company of others before whom he feels inferior. The salesman has obtained temporary forcefulness to press through a sale and persuade his customer. The journalist has overcome his reserve and gets the information he needs. However, in the process, the alcohol which reduced the tension has become a drug of addiction, bringing its own train of physical damage. The alcoholic drinks to feel better, but this alleviation leads to a new and progressive disease.

I would suggest that we can regard those who seek our help as people who were in a marginal state before contacting us. When we see them they suffer from anxiety, usually obvious but sometimes masked. We need to understand the *precipitating situation*, the event in their current life experience which produced the change in their usual ability to hold the different parts of their personality together, to manage the discrepant segments of their lives.

We have to go further than this. We have to understand the *previous balance* which existed before the crack-up occurred. However precariously, these people had been balanced at a level of relative independence. However stressful their existence, they could manage. If we are to be expert in the help we offer, we need the

103

ability and skills to comprehend exactly the organization that previously they could achieve.

We do this by interviewing. We allow the person in crisis to talk about the actual conditions of his personal life, conveying not only how the crisis arose but also how this person came to be in the state of readiness for that particular crisis.

This comprehending of the previous balance, a technical procedure which can be carried out by competent helpers, may be called *diagnosis of the personality state*. It will be obvious to us that the helping steps we undertake will vary according to the personality which we discover in our client or patient.

I want now to consider briefly the main form of help which we are in the position to offer, and I will also indicate the harm we can do.

Ventilation (or catharsis) is a procedure by which a person is enabled to express in words and feeling his current difficulties. We attempt to reduce the pressure he is under; in a sense, we enable him to let off steam. The interviewer's task is to participate in the interview, and, at the same time, to observe carefully what is taking place. A competent interviewer shows this dual ability: the troubled person sees that what he says is heard with interest, but, at the same time, the interviewer is also busy methodically obtaining information with which to make sense of the encounter.

An interviewer is alertly aware that he can be helpful to the distressed person, but equally he can be extremely harmful. A successful interview must be a constructive experience for the sufferer, affording him relief and insight; for the interviewer it is also a technical exercise enabling him to obtain necessary knowledge.

An expert also knows the limitations of his approach, the extent to which he is in a position to be helpful. I have stressed that our skill lies in relieving people's pressures by enabling them to talk, freely and confidentially, knowing that we will listen calmly and try not to respond with our own pet enthusiasms but in accordance with the needs of the person we are aiming to assist. We do not strive to impose our own plans or hopes on our patient or client.

Our objective is to set the person on his feet: rather, to help him to put himself on his feet. We do this by means of a third technical step. In our enquiry we set out to discover what the person's assets are, his habitual strength and skills, the sources of his comfort, the areas of reassurance in his life. These are the psychological measures which in the past he could call on himself to neutralize anxiety when it occurred. A skilled interviewer is able to discern these strengths, these positive attributes in the personality of a distressed person even at a time of crisis, and help the creative sides of his nature. These are the integrating tendencies. Usually they are associated with positive feeling: affection for a parent, love for one's children, pride in a skill or a talent.

Our chief harm will arise from failure to recognize when we are dealing with more serious illness, which will not be relieved by our interest and the discussion we allow to develop. We need to recognize which cases need medical care. We must know what the illness of depression looks like, and enable the patient to find suitable treatment. We must proceed immediately to have suicidal people placed in suitable medical care. We must enable alcoholics ready for treatment to reach proper treatment services. Achieving these ends calls for constant communication between the Samaritan organization and the medical profession.

Lay organizations and suicide prevention

Professor Erwin Stengel
Co-President of The Samaritans

In the prevention of suicide, medical men are working side by side with non-medical people and organizations; and the success of their endeavours depends on their close co-operation. It is, therefore, important that we know what each of us can contribute to the common aim and that there should be no misunderstandings among us. I sometimes come across psychiatrists who mistrust lay people and organizations engaged in suicide prevention, and some of the latter seem to have wrong ideas about the doctor's contribution. Only by airing these misunderstandings can we prevent friction which would do harm to the common purpose.

The approach of The Samaritans has a special appeal to me because it is concerned with aspects of the suicide problem in which I have been particularly interested. Naturally, my approach will differ somewhat from that of a minister of the church and the lay person, but we all are agreed about the sanctity of human life. I am sure that the psychiatrist can learn a great deal from their observations, if only because their clientele is probably not quite the same as his.

Psychiatrists have, of course, for some time now been interested in the role of mental illness in the causation of suicide. Not more than one-third of the people who kill themselves have been found to be psychiatric patients, but this does not mean that the remaining two-thirds consist of well-balanced, mentally normal persons—far from it: they had not been seen by a psychiatrist although many of them ought to have been.

I have so far been talking about suicides, not about attempted suicides. But are they not the same type of people, differing only by the outcome? Do we not, therefore, speak of successful and unsuccessful suicidal attempts? And does not everything that applies to the suicides also apply to the suicidal attempts? Are not the people who turn to The Samaritans those who might have swelled the numbers of the suicides if they had not sought their help? The answer to all these questions is "Perhaps", or, more honestly, "We don't know." In talking about the suicide rate and its reduction we are referring to the dead. Only a fraction of the people who are seen by The Samaritans later kill themselves. I understand that they form less than one per cent of their clients.

Then we have the large number of people who attempted suicide. If we compare this group with that of the suicides, we find that the two groups differ significantly in many respects, although it often depends on accidental circumstances outside the individual's control whether his body is taken to the mortuary or whether he finds himself in hospital, or whether the incident is hushed up without even a doctor being called in. Attempted suicides are on the average younger than the suicides, they have not a male but a female majority, and the proportion of people mentally or physically ill among them is probably smaller than in the suicide group. Only a small proportion of them finally die from their own hands. The figures vary between one and ten per cent after five to ten years. Although this is only a small minority, it is a much greater proportion of suicides than we find if we follow up people who have not made suicidal attempts. We have, then, two different groups: those who commit and those who attempt suicide. The two groups differ in size and slightly overlap, because a proportion of the bigger group enters the smaller in the course of time.

Where do the clients of The Samaritans come in? I should very much like to know. As a group they may differ from both the suicide and the attempted suicide groups. The people who contemplate suicide are a very complex population which is probably greater than the suicide and attempted suicide group put together. Their number can never be known, because many do not communicate their intention to anybody, others mention it only to those close to them, while others again tend to communicate it to outsiders who offer help. The clients of The Samaritans come from the last mentioned section. It would help research into the suicide problem if certain data about them, such as sex, civil status (single, married, divorced, widowed), socio-economic status, religious affiliation, etc., could be obtained.[1]

In the meantime, we cannot be certain how much good organizations such as The Samaritans are doing in terms of figures. Possibly we shall never know pre-

[1] The Association has now adopted a new Standard Report Form with a tear-off slip allowing these statistics to be separated from personal details of clients.—Ed.

cisely. But do not let this worry us unduly. Ministers of the church are in the same position, and so are doctors in many fields of their work. They, like the Samaritans, do what they are doing not only because they believe that it will help their clients, but because they have to do it.

I should like to warn against incautious use of statistics. There is a temptation to test the value of the work of The Samaritans and similar organizations by the rise and fall of the suicide figures. This could be quite misleading. The factors on which the suicide rate depends are so numerous that we cannot relate them to one particular factor unless all the others are identical in the groups we compare. Statistics are risky, because it may even make the Samaritans doubt, quite unjustly, the value of their work. I should like to illustrate what I mean. Sheffield has no Samaritan branch.[1] It has had a very low suicide rate compared with other industrial communities, some of which already have a Samaritan branch. If such a branch should be created at Sheffield and the suicide rate should show a further decrease, the newly founded Samaritan branch may be inclined to attribute this to their efforts. But if the suicide rate should happen to go up a year or two after the new branch was established, are we going to attribute this to the Samaritans also? Unless they want to have it both ways, which they cannot, they ought not to worry about statistics. This can only get them into trouble with the experts. Their work does not need any such vindication because it fulfils a need which common

[1] The Sheffield Branch was started soon after this paper was read.—Ed.

humanity as well as scientific research have recognized as essential.

In offering help to those who contemplate suicide, the Samaritans are trying to forestall the appeal effect of the suicidal attempt and indeed of suicide. They are trying to tell those people, "See, you can have friendship and love without risking your life." However, lack of a friend is not the only cause of suicidal intentions. There are quite a few others. This brings me to the doctors' role in the prevention of suicide.

I should like to discuss the following questions: (1) Who are the people in despair and with suicidal intention whom the doctor sees? (2) What does the doctor do for them? (3) Who are the people in despair and with thoughts of suicide whom the doctor ought to see? I am not distinguishing here between the psychiatrist and the general practitioner, because the latter has to deal with the majority of emotionally disturbed people.

The first question was which of the large number who are in despair and are thinking of suicide go to the doctor? He will, of course, see most of those who are physically ill. Physical illness plays an important part in the causation of many suicides, especially among the elderly. He will also see those who are mentally ill in the narrow sense, although some types of mental illness, especially abnormal depressions, are not easily distinguishable from what the lay person may regard as a normal though somewhat excessive depression. I include the neuroses among mental illness, although the majority of neurotics and quite a few people suffering from a serious mental illness do not see the doctor when they ought to. The doctor is also called in when people get into trouble with the law because of misconduct caused by abnormal drives.

The doctor, then, is dealing only with a minority of people who suffer from some sort of mental disorder, because the others do not consult him. Reading the literature of The Samaritans, one would think that it is easy to define what is the doctor's and what is the Samaritan's field of activity. This is not so. First of all, what do we mean by mental or psychological illness? Certainly not only those conditions which used to be called the insanities. If we include the neurotics, as we must, we are dealing probably with about one-third of the population. If we also include the abnormal personalities the proportion is even higher. Psychiatry used to be defined as the study and treatment of mental diseases. This definition no longer describes the scope of modern psychiatry, which is now more correctly defined as the study and treatment of abnormal behaviour.

What does the doctor, and especially the psychiatrist, do for those of his patients who are in despair and are thinking of suicide? Some he may have to send to a mental hospital, but the majority are treated in surgeries and out-patient clinics. Some are given physical treatments, many are treated with drugs, but most of them are receiving or ought to receive some kind of psychotherapy, which means that their individual problems are ventilated and if possible the patients are helped in solving those difficulties. Whenever appropriate and possible, the doctor will gladly avail himself of the help of a social worker, of a minister of the church, and of sympathetic relatives or friends of the patient.

The doctor's work does not consist mainly of cutting, shocking and drugging. In fact, what has been called the doctor-patient relationship is often the most powerful and effective method at his disposal. It plays a part in the treatment of every case, whatever the illness may be. The Samaritans' definition of 'befriending' excludes professionals, but in a looser sense it has always been a part of the doctor's functions. The doctor, then, is or ought to be a Samaritan with medical and medico-psychological knowledge and skills. I do not mean that all the clients of The Samaritans ought to see a doctor or even a psychiatrist, instead of a lay helper, but I cannot accept the idea of the doctor as an impersonal detached scientist. It is true that his relationship to his patients must not become too personal, but the same is true for the minister of the church and the Samaritan. All of us are, in our relationship to our clients, at the same time more and less than our private selves. All of us will get into trouble if we forget this.

The third question was who the people in despair and with thoughts of suicide are, who ought to be seen by a doctor. The logical answer is all those for whom a doctor could do more than a lay person. But are there not plenty of normal people who are contemplating suicide? It all depends on what we mean by normal. I have never failed to find on closer examination symptoms of mental disorders or of an abnormal personality in a person who threatened or had attempted suicide. I am excluding here suicidal acts committed by people exposed to extraordinary stresses which do not arise from the common vicissitudes of life. However, the question, what is normal, is theoretical rather than practical, because only a minority of those who contemplate suicide consult psychiatrists. If all did, we certainly could not cope with them—and there will never be enough doctor's time available for all abnormal people in despair. Anybody who is concerned with human relations can help those people as long as he is aware of his limitations.

Most Samaritans have been aware of their limitations, and they have kept in close touch with doctors, especially with psychiatrists. We certainly need their help in our fight against suicide. The Samaritans' main task is to receive messages of help from people in despair and to respond to them. In many cases first aid treatment will be sufficient, while others will require 'befriending'. It is important for the lay helpers to realize whose place they are taking in trying to help their clients. They are not standing in for the doctor nor for the minister of religion, but for a member of the family which acts as a source of strength and as a refuge in times of crisis. We can assume that if their clients had parents or brothers or sisters to turn to, or a friend who functions in their place, they would not have to turn to the Samaritans. If we define their role in this way, the problem, which of their clients should be referred to a doctor, or a social worker, or a minister of religion, will be as easy, or as difficult, as it would be if the person concerned was a member of one's family. In both situations one will have to rely on informed common sense and on intuition helped by whatever experience of similar situations one may have.

The mystique of the Samaritan method

Dr. Richard Fox
Hon. Psychiatric Consultant to The Samaritans

There are essential differences between what I do as a Consultant Psychiatrist and what Samaritans do themselves. I am sent patients by other agencies—usually the family doctor, I do not take them straight off the streets as Samaritans do. I have a letter of referral and often other documents which give the background of the disorder. Samaritans usually have nothing except what the client tells them, which may be accurate or may not. If someone wants to see me he makes an appointment (which may be weeks ahead) and will be at a place of my choosing. All very unSamaritan-like. There are medical emergency services: the family doctor is contracted to supply them and can be fined for leaving his practice unattended, but not, of course, for being out on his rounds for a couple of hours. The family doctor can call the specialist urgently to a patient's home—which happens to me about two days out of three. But one has clinics to do and Conferences to attend. My hospital always has at least two doctors on duty, but they cannot always be traced at once, and it is up to a quarter of a mile from some parts to the nearest outside telephone.

These are important differences, and of course the Good Samaritan did not content himself with giving the

115

injured traveller an appointment for the Jerusalem
County Hospital for Friday fortnight at 2.45 p.m. I
make no excuses for myself, I may say. When one is
medically responsible for 200 in-patients, and copes
with over a thousand out-patient attendances a year
plus those home visits I mentioned, one must have
organization. My hospital is the base for a psychiatric
service in Essex and Herts that runs from Canvey
Island to Steeple Bumpstead and from Hertford to
Harwich. The thought of being personally, instantly
accessible to all of the three-quarter million-odd
people living there is frightening.

So the first part of the mystique is obviously instant
availability. And do not think too badly of us non-Sam-
aritans when we cannot always be located in a hurry.

The next major difference between us is what we do
with our client or patient when he finally breaks through
to us. He may go to the Samaritans for all sorts of
reasons, but what they have to offer above all is *friendship*. He comes to me for advice, consultation, treatment.
I am the specialist with my name on the door. I am up
there, on my sort of metaphorical throne. The psychiatric patient bares his soul to me just as the medical
patient bares his chest to the physician. Even if he is the
local Lord Mayor, the patient is at a psychological
disadvantage in that he is coming to me for help. I run
the interview, I ask the questions. He is quite likely to be
profusely grateful that a busy man like myself will grant
him 7½ minutes of my time after a wait of only an hour
and a half. This relationship with the fatherly doctor and
the motherly nurse carries echoes of the patient's
parent-child memories. The barrier that this situation

creates can hinder treatment. The patient can be so in awe of the doctor that he dare not say things he fears the doctor may not like, as for example that the tablets made him feel worse. He chucks them down the sink and battles on grimly. Or not. Perceptive doctors try to overcome some of those difficulties by putting comfortable armchairs in the waiting rooms, shoving the desk to the side of the room instead of having it between themselves and the patient, and removing badges of office, like white coats bulging with instruments—hammers, rubber-tubes and so on.

But, however informal one tries to be, this is a professional relationship and one does not take one's patients out for coffee, give them one's home telephone number (mine is ex-directory), write them little affectionate letters in one's own handwriting and make oneself available at all times of the day and night. The relationship may be warm, it may be intense, it may have all kinds of deep psychological meanings which have to be brought out and discussed, but the game is played according to fairly strict rules. Above all the doctor is trained (or should be, for not all are) to recognize the way in which attachments can build up between patient and therapist which have symbolic meaning in terms of the past relationship of both of them with their early parent-figures. We give this the technical term 'transference', meaning transferred emotion, for the patient's attitude to the therapist, and 'counter transference' when the therapist becomes involved with the patient. If one allows a friend to turn himself into a patient one loses the friend—however much good one may do him.

I do not say that friendship and a professional treatment relationship are mutually exclusive—rules are made to be broken—but it is the very exceptional patient and therapist who can handle such explosive possibilities. All this is far from the Samaritan mystique of befriending which *must not probe* into things the way the therapist does. To probe can represent 'psychological seduction' and can be a hazardous business. So Samaritans must realize that there are things that their Method just cannot manage, just as I realize that there are plenty of things *my* Method cannot manage. The lesson is that they and I must have a clear idea of what we are each trying to do, and not hesitate to cross-refer cases where necessary. The Samaritan mystique is in many ways more demanding than my own, though it calls less on training and more on broad human qualities.

One of the most crucial features in the Samaritan relationship is the acceptance by the befriender of negative, unpleasant features in the client. We all of us have a nasty side buried—or not buried—somewhere, and troubled people who come for help will from time to time show attitudes or behaviour personally repugnant to the one who helps. The 'certain man' who lay by the side of the road when the Good Samaritan passed by was evidently not a pleasant sight, covered, one supposes, with blood, dirt and flies. And that is life. The Samaritan volunteer with pretty ideas of what clients ought to be like had better look for other forms of service. In an introductory talk on sex to our local group I deliberately made things rather nasty in places, and as expressions of horror passed over the faces of the more upright of the local citizens I explained that these things may be nasty, but they existed, and that sooner or later Samaritan workers would meet up with some of these things. Repugnance against sexual deviations was common enough, I said, particularly in our sexually-inhibited culture, and was not itself grounds for seeking psychiatric treatment. But they were going to get clients who felt they must unburden themselves of their guilt about, say, homosexuality, and any volunteer who felt that he could not face this should think very seriously whether he ought to be entering this work at all.

One must be prepared to accept the whole person, not just the nice bits, without falling victim to the Scylla of outraged horror, or the Charybdis of licentious curiosity. The sexually deviated are used to ostracism to the point where they assume it when none exists—a paranoid reaction, as we call it, but based all too often on real and bitter experience. Any nuance of disgust or rejection in the befriender will be picked up, and the client may go forth in sadness thinking that the Samaritan is "just like all the rest".

The opposite error takes various forms. There is the befriender (or therapist), for example, with ill-adjusted sexual problems himself who urges the client (or patient) into more and more elaborate accounts of all that he has done, with whom and how, getting thereby some vicarious erotic satisfaction himself. This is the lascivious "Tell me more" approach, which is a form of voyeurism. Or the befriender who hastens to ill-judged reassurance, making light of a disorder which the client knows all too well is of the greatest gravity. Some acts are wrong when judged from almost any social, rational or religious point of view, and a befriender who says that they are not is being hypocritical and will forfeit the trust of his client. Or the befriender who thinks he can give support by baring his own soul in return. This is perhaps the commonest pitfall, the "I have suffered too, old chap" approach. I do not say one must *never* do it, but I do regard it as fraught with danger. To start with, the client has quite enough troubles of his own, without taking on another's. Then there is the risk that he will lose confidence in a person who is evidently troubled as badly as he is. I learned my lesson some years ago, just after qualifying, when I shared some rather personal matters in an effort to relieve a young patient in much distress, but who then passed on everything I had said with much gusto to every nurse and doctor that she met. But Alcoholics Anonymous, and similar organizations, work, of course, on the basis that the members help each other by sharing their past experiences. The risk of mutually-shared distress is probably much less great at the friendship level than in the patient/therapist situation. It is the Counseller who must particularly beware of, as it were, going naked into the vestry or consulting room.

Finally, there is the client whose unconscious motive is to gain attention and fuss, to produce a shock effect, and who will plumb greater and greater depths of degradation—in a masochistic sort of way, perhaps—until he *does* produce some response in his befriender. One thinks of the good old days of the Salvation Army when the Alleluyas mounted in enthusiasm as the public confession became blacker and blacker. (And the handout afterwards, as it were, became correspondingly larger.)

What no Samaritan can expect, of course, is the reward which the client can offer by way of gratitude. It is nice when one's patients offer their thanks, but rather exceptional. By and large people hate being ill, they hate having to go for help and putting themselves in a rather humiliating way into the hands of others. This hate often spills over, in the irrational way that the mind works, on to the person that they go to for help, and one must be aware always of this under-current of hostility—of ambivalent feelings—which can interfere with treatment. Or with befriending. Hostility is often part of the 'transferred emotions', again, formerly directed towards the parent or parent-figure: the 'negative transference', as we call it then. The Samaritan who has done a good job can expect a kind word from the Director. Any gratitude from the client is a bonus. Once again, I would expect that the hostility factor may be less of a problem at the level of friendship than in the treatment situation.

These are exceedingly difficult problems in which reading articles or listening to talks can act as no more than signposts. Every road has different, uncharted turnings, and learning to drive is a long and tedious business. Trial and error is one way of learning, but an instructor can often save one from going straight into the canal. The golden rule, in so far as there is one, is to be sympathetic but uncommitted, to listen with com-passion but without judgment. To avoid giving advice as far as possible, particularly when it is unasked. It is *not* the Samaritan's job to tell the client to change his job, divorce his wife or invest in Unit Trusts. One must remember always the undercurrent of hostility. *Whatever* you advise is likely to be wrong, and then it is *your fault.*

Troubled people divide themselves into three broad groups (which overlap a bit at the fringes). There are the *psychotics*, who have lost touch with reality as we know it, who believe that they have committed imaginary sins, who hear voices, or believe that they are acting under the influence of rays from outer space. Paradoxically, these most seriously ill people are the easiest to handle when one knows how. Then there is the much larger group of *neurotics* who punish themselves with irrational anxieties, tensions and fears, but who remain in touch with reality—a group which shades off at all points into the 'normal'. Depressions fall into both groups. These are in turn easier to handle than the last group of *personality disorders*, in which deeply-seated deviant character traits are present to excess. This group shades off into the normal even more than the neurotic—anyone looked at hard enough can be seen as having some kind of personality disorder. The group embraces the whole wealth of human personality and takes in those who are too active or not active enough, too withdrawn or too outgoing, too lazy, too demanding, too unreliable, too badtempered, too fussy, too timid, etc., etc., etc. But it is the group termed *psychopathic* that bothers us the most—a term which has come, in England, to imply persistent social irresponsibility or actual antisocial conduct with or without undue aggressiveness. The neurotic punishes himself, the psychopath punishes everyone else. He or she may do it overtly by smashing things up or robbing mail trains, or covertly by sowing difficulty and discord. He turns friends into enemies, employees against employer, doctor against nurse, Samaritan Worker against Director—or vice-versa. This is unconsciously motivated, manipulative behaviour. The psychopath does not know why he is doing it and may not even know that he is doing it at all—these things seem to be rooted in complex distorted childhood experiences, perhaps allied to delay in maturation of parts of the brain. Certainly it is hard to call them 'sinful'. But it presents a tremendous problem to those to whom the psychopath turns for help—and the help he *really* wants is not usually what it appears at first sight: the man at my out-patient clinic, for example, who presented as a very convincing suicidal depression but who recovered overnight after admission and stayed in for as long as he possibly could—to avoid his creditors, as we subsequently found out. The psychopath will inveigle his befriender or therapist into all sorts of situations—he will try to enlist his help against his spouse, his landlord, his former employers (usually a large number of these), against the National Assistance Board, the Employment Exchange, the Children's Department—even against the Police. He will ask for loans which he has no intention of repaying.

The hazards here are enormous. It is easy for even experienced people to be deceived by the plausibility of the client, and determined attempts to help can lead to an impossible increase in the demands made on one, and later an intense, negative, hostile reaction when the demands are not met. The mystique with the predominantly inadequate client is through friendship to help him face real life and shoulder his responsibilities, not for the Samaritan to shoulder them for him, because this may foster dependency and increase the client's inadequacy. The more malignant psychopath will abuse even this, and will attack a Samaritan where he is weakest: by making suicide threats. If one still does not respond, he may act out one of these threats by a calculated suicide bid causing the greatest possible commotion, fuss and bother, and with the least possible danger to life. Patients arrive at the hospital gate with bags packed saying that they have just taken five aspirin. It is exceptionally rare for such a psychopath to kill himself, though there is always the possibility of accident. Just as the young doctor must learn with sadness that he cannot cure everyone, so must the young Samaritan realize, without losing too much sleep, that there are those whom his mystique, however mysterious, cannot help, and that unskilled attempts to do so may rebound on both him and his client. The Samaritan Director and Psychiatric Consultant must keep in the closest touch with the befriender where predominantly psychopathic conduct is suspected. The main difficulty in recognizing this is, as I mentioned, that psychopathic conduct shades off at all points of the compass into the normal. Clearly, we must not allow fears of the destructive psychopath to paralyse our efforts to help those who are on the fringes of the disorder.

One could, if one had the wisdom, talk endlessly of the pitfalls that await one in one's relationships with others—it is a book of life. Frankly, after nine years in psychiatry and six in other branches of medicine, plus six years of medical training, I know that I am still a beginner. Pablo Casals, surely one of the greatest cellists that ever lived, said recently—in his eighties—that he practised diligently every day and, he thought, continued to make progress. One can but try to emulate that.

One last difficult topic awaits. The mystique may be, in some ways, a bit *too* mysterious. In these methodical days we are taught to look at what we do to the point of conducting operational research, and there are few aspects of life so far unmeasured by the stop-watches of Organization and Management teams. And one must admit that the benefits of such studies have been enormous. Medical treatment has been no exception to the pan-scientific trend, and in few centres is the word of the Professor accepted as sufficient evidence for truth, as once it was. Hard, verifiable facts are what is wanted. This can mean treating one group of people with drug A and comparing their progress with a carefully-matched group given drug B or dummy tablets made to look just like drug A. Experience has shown that to avoid results which are biased in various ways, it is necessary for the patient, for the nurse, and for the doctor all to be unaware of what the tablets contain until the trial period is over and the code can be broken. There are many safeguards, of course, to protect the patients and no one nowadays need fear that he may be 'experimented on' without his knowing.

The application of the controlled trial, as it is called, has led to incalculable benefits for the whole of humanity —it underlies, for example, the virtual elimination of

T.B. as a health hazard. The standard treatment, both expensive and distressing, for a certain kind of cancer was found to kill people off faster and less pleasantly than did the untreated disease. And so on.

Now I doubt if Samaritan work is susceptible to an O. & M. approach, and nor is it likely that a Samaritan Director would take kindly to a controlled evaluation study. I suppose clients could be chosen at random and either taken on for befriending or told to go away, with comparison of the outcome in the two groups. But people *are* asking with increasing pressure four questions: *what* sort of people come, *why* do they come, *what* do you do to help them, and above all *what are the results*? We have an idea about questions one and three, and Samaritans are trying now with a new form to answer question two, though one may doubt the accuracy and comparability, branch to branch, of data. But we really do not have any idea about results. It seems to me that if we are to place Samaritan work on a firm foundation and expect support from hard-headed, wealthy benefactors, if we are going to attract the right sort of volunteer, and if we are going to broaden our knowledge, refine our techniques of befriending and learn to help people more effectively, then some sort of evaluation study must come. Some break is needed in the follow-up taboo, so that ex-clients can be seen after a year, two years, three years, maybe, to help us learn from our mistakes. I am not questioning the transparent worth of the whole Samaritan enterprise—I think there can be no two views about that—but I *am* urging that a way be found to learn how to do a good job even better.

Loneliness, sexual difficulties and guilt

Dr. W. Lawton Tonge
Hon. Psychiatric Consultant to the Sheffield Samaritans

However we may wish to define mental health, there is one fact which cannot be denied about healthy people: they are continuously supported in a network of personal relationships. Conversely, the lives of suicides and would-be suicides show to a greater or lesser degree an interruption or disturbance of their relationships. These relationships can of course be broken in many ways and for many reasons.

From our point of view, loneliness, sexual difficulties and guilt are three facets of this problem. All reflect or imply some degree of interpersonal failure. While it may be convenient for me to deal with them separately, it will be understood that there is a good deal of common ground both in our understanding of these problems and in our response to them.

Usually, when one speaks of loneliness, I find that most people are thinking of social, that is physical, isolation. "I have no one to talk to . . ." the clients complain. This is a very real problem, especially for the old and for strangers. If one has survived the death of friends and family, there may literally be no one left with whom there are any bonds of friendship. Equally distressing is the plight of younger people who have immigrated into a city and spend long hours in the bed-sitter. It is well known that such situations predispose to suicide. Sainsbury, for example, found that suicide was much more common amongst the unemployed, lodging-house keepers and domestic servants. This is not just a question of social class: according to the Registrar General, miners share the lowest suicide rate, together with clergymen.

Sainsbury then studied the way of life, and found that nearly a third of his suicides were living alone, and over a fifth lived in boarding houses: and these are much higher proportions than in the general population of London. This suggested that isolation, loneliness and not-belonging were perhaps important motives for suicide. This would explain why lonely occupations, such as domestic service and lodging-house keeping, have high suicide rates, while occupations which bring men into close contact with each other, such as miners and the clergy, have low suicide rates.

In order to check this hypothesis, Sainsbury examined those London boroughs which had high suicide rates, and compared them with boroughs with low suicide rates. As one might expect, he found that in boroughs with a high suicide rate there was a much increased proportion of persons living alone, especially living in one room and in hotels and lodgings. They also had a greater number of immigrants, and a greater number of people born outside London. The rates for divorce and illegitimacy were also higher where suicide was prevalent. The facts are no longer in dispute: to be exposed to the stress of isolation and loneliness increases the risk of suicide.

Faced with this situation, it is obvious that our response must be to meet this need, in so far as we are able. In our own clinic we became disturbed by this plight of older women living on their own, and we started a social club for them. Although it was only possible for the club to meet once a week, the response on the part of our patients was most gratifying: their need to attend hospital or have treatment as in-patients fell off markedly. Depression was the most common and severe symptom, but our simple institution, undemanding in time and money for its organizers, now makes some contribution to the prophylaxis of suicide for this socially underprivileged population.

For the same reason, it is no coincidence that the volunteers in The Samaritans are called 'befrienders'. Human beings need the support of friendly relationships as surely as they need food and water, and deprivation in this respect can lead equally to a fatal result. There are few of us who, at some time or other in our life, are not tempted to despair and suicide, and the knowledge that there is someone who cares for us is a strong barrier to the impulses of self-destruction. The provision of this friendly support must therefore be one of the major concerns of any organization which is engaged in the prevention of suicide.

But I am convinced that neither a supply of befrienders, however generous, nor the provision of social clubs, is an adequate answer to the problem of human loneliness. Loneliness not as a social fact but as an inner experience is a word with more than one meaning.

The experience of loneliness is probably inseparable from life as we know it today. Indeed loneliness in the form of privacy is a very highly rated commodity. At least in this country we pay extra for houses which are completely detached from our neighbours, for gardens which cannot be overlooked. For many holiday-makers, the perfect beach is one which is devoid of any other people. This is one aspect of contemporary culture which is in marked contrast with earlier times. Paul Halmos, in his study of solitude and privacy, quotes Rosamund Bagne-Powell: "We must remember that overcrowding was characteristic of the age. Well-to-do people thought little of . . . two sleeping in a bed. The pupils at expensive boarding schools were herded together under the most insanitary conditions. Servants slept in the kitchen or lay on the staircase and passages. Travellers at inns would share rooms and beds with total strangers. Privacy did not seem to be valued even by those who could insist upon it."

There were, of course, many good practical reasons for this avoidance of solitude; by and large it was dangerous. Public security could not be taken for granted as it is today. Moreover, the whole structure of feudal society demanded that one should be placed in a certain station in life, to which one was bound with duties and privileges, and from which there was no escape. To rise in the world, as we know it, was unthinkable, and to be an independent operator was madness. As Lewis Mumford puts it: "The unattached person during the middle ages was one either condemned to exile or doomed to death: if alive, he immediately sought to attach himself, at least to a band of robbers. To exist, one had to belong to an association: a household, a manor, a monastery, a guild:

there was no security except in association, and no freedom that did not recognize the obligations of a corporate life. One lived and died in the style of one's class and corporation." But today this solitude which we seek may also be the loneliness which we fear. It represents a need which is also a hazard characteristic of our times.

The meaning of this loneliness is most clearly marked out in the case of a young woman who consulted me in depression and despair. Her temperament was that of lively, careless, extraverted person. Her parents were careful middle-class people who hoped above all that their daughter would hold a steady and respectable job in some sort of secretarial capacity which would be completely in conformity with the family tradition. Loyally this girl had sought to live up to the expectations of her family, but found that she was encircled by a sense of frustration and despair. Her friends, most of whom shared the outlook of her parents, could not fathom the cause of her unhappiness. When pressed, she admitted that it was her secret ambition to work as a receptionist in an hotel or club, but she felt she did not dare mention this at home because it was so contrary to her parents' ambitions for her; likewise her friends would not understand. She felt lonely, deserted and in despair, and yet I would hesitate to diagnose this as a neurotic problem.

I have dwelt at some length on this somewhat everyday example because I think it illustrates clearly a characteristically contemporary dilemma. The need for self-determination, the right to control one's own affairs, is highly valued in our culture, whether for individuals or for nations. Yet this decision demands more or less of a break with the past. Old ways may have to be rejected. This can lead to great feelings of loneliness, and is a sort of separation anxiety: the spiritual equivalent of the panic which small children feel when they cry out for their mother and get no reply. In much the same way the young people of our society cry out for guidance and are met by the silence of moral condemnation or the exhortation to work things out for themselves. I suggest therefore that the struggle for emotional maturity inevitably brings about some degree of loneliness. One has lost touch with the older generation, and one's own generation has yet to find an answer. There is no one to turn to.

But there are other and more intractable forms of loneliness than the isolation of an individual in a crisis of self-determination. I see loneliness essentially as the consequence of a breakdown in the emotional transactions between people. The most impenetratable isolation is when the person concerned finds himself unable to enter into an emotional commitment, notwithstanding an intense desire to do so. Such people find themselves lonely although surrounded by friends and family. Perhaps married, they find themselves committed to a life of pretending to feelings which they do not experience, and, which is the more bitter, because they have to simulate feelings which they ardently wish to be real. When faced with this type of loneliness, it is tempting to ascribe it to circumstances; thus some women imagine that a lover would be more successful than their husband in breaking down their inner reserve; some unmarried men believe that their failure to marry is because they do not move in the right social circles, and so on. But in their innermost hearts they know these thoughts to be but rationalizations, and that a crystal wall, transparent and infrangible, effectively seals their hearts against those who could love them.

This is a neurotic situation which responds, if at all, to psychotherapy, and I believe it is beyond the reach of counselling or befriending. However, the act of befriending, although powerless to shatter their invisible defences against love, does something to relieve the acute sense of loneliness and frustration which these neurotics suffer. To know that someone is trying to get through induces a pathetic gratitude, although the result is known to be useless.

This is not the time or place to discuss in any depth the psychopathology of these conditions, but it must be remarked that in many of these cases, underneath a façade of friendliness and sophistication is a deep mistrust. A typical comment from one of my patients was that he had learned not to pray to God because if he made his wants known, that would make sure they would be refused. Such people are often generous as regards their belongings, and their time, provided that they are not personally involved. In their own deepest needs, they are unable to give and are therefore often frigid or impotent in their sexual relationships. Although desperately wanting the love of others, their fear of involvement closes their eyes to the opportunities for love relationships which are presented to them. They are constantly exposed to humiliations when they see others, less talented, to be more successful both in love and work.

The same difficulties and frustrations attend their

treatment. Although they make conscientious patients, they never really trust the therapist, and complain that he does not offer the help to which they are entitled. They are quick to take offence and do not believe that their therapist is really concerned for them. These invisible barriers are very hard to break, and bring humiliation to the patient and frustration to the therapist.

Although the situation which I have described is fortunately rare, I believe that minor varieties of this difficulty are common enough in many who complain of loneliness. Behind the rationalization of lack of social contact and bad luck, one can dimly perceive the scared and humiliated ego which draws back at every attempt on the part of others for a closer relationship. In their hearts these people live in a barren, deserted and hostile world.

But there are other forms of loneliness, in which social and psychological factors are both involved. I am referring especially to the homosexual in the United Kingdom. I know that this country is not alone in its persecution of (male) homosexuals—I have never been clear as to why homosexual activity between adult consenting females in private should be less immoral, but that apparently is the view that our legislators take.

Homosexuality is not an uncommon condition. Kinsey estimates that it amounts to four per cent of the male population. The aetiology of the condition is obscure, but, almost certainly, genetic, psychological and social factors enter into each case in varying degrees of importance. What is less certain is that about only one in twenty-five achieve heterosexuality. Even when psychological treatment is offered, one is sometimes left with the impression, as in one of my own cases, that cure is spontaneous rather than due to treatment.

It is not easy to appreciate the plight of these men. Although some are capable of heterosexual activity, it is my impression that they are not capable of accepting sustaining love from a woman: sexual intercourse is for them a physical not an emotional outlet. The majority find little pleasure in the company of women. Their male friendships are no easier. The attractive man they meet in the bar may well turn out to be a crook or, worse, a blackmailer. The constant pressure of society's censure tends to make their lives unstable and their sexual contacts promiscuous. The more mature may settle down to more or less stable liaisons, but even there the fear of exposure is never absent. Apart from the risk of social and legal consequences, the more sensitive of them are plagued with a feeling of guilt. They know that they belong to an unacceptable deviation and feel themselves to be outcasts of society. This applies even to homosexuals who have refrained from sexual activity. Indeed, the chaste men are afraid of any friendship with their own sex, in case an element of impurity (as they would term it) creeps in.

The inner shame of being judged guilty by their own conscience is probably the more important reason for their loneliness than society's disapproval, although I would warn you against underestimating the social pressures against homosexuality in this country. Either way, it is no wonder that homosexuals are lonely people, prone to sudden panics and despair and vulnerable to impulses of suicide.

Guilt and sexuality are common bedfellows in our culture. The process of bringing up children implies the development of a system of control in their personalities. Disciplined and successful endeavour in adult life necessarily implies the restriction of wayward impulses. The lack of control which infants display in respect of their feelings and impulses would make organized life impossible if adults behaved in the same way. This is true not only of sophisticated societies but also in the most primitive cultures. The romantic idea of the noble savage, untrammelled by convention, is not confirmed by the anthropologists. Illiterate cultures carry as many taboos and prohibitions as our own, although they are sometimes strikingly different.

I make these general remarks because the view is expressed in some quarters that psychiatry, and especially psychoanalysis, is opposed to any internal restraint on behaviour. Nothing could be further from the truth. But this does not stop us from criticizing some of the prohibitions in our own culture which are both irrational and unhelpful to mental health.

The association between sexuality and guilt in our own culture leads to some strange consequences. It is clearly the cause in many cases of sexual failure—either impotency or frigidity—but such cases I feel require medical attention. Very often, the moral condemnation of sexual activity on the part of parents seems to encourage just that behaviour which the parents are at pains to prevent.

I am certain, for example, that many cases of promiscuity and illegitimate pregnancy in young girls are motivated by spite towards their mothers rather than by excessive and uncontrolled libido. Children who are reared in a moral atmosphere which associates sexuality with guilt often find, when they reach adult life, that sexual behaviour is only exciting when it takes place in a guilty context, and this applies as much to extramarital as to premarital behaviour. How many frigid women, to take another example, do not also commit adultery? Certainly many of them are tempted. Their explanation is that they wished to find out if their sexual difficulties would persist in an extramarital affair (their implication here is that the husband is somehow at fault) but I suspect that this is a rationalization. It seems to me more likely that their guilty feelings about sex prohibit sexual activity at home, but they are free to enjoy sex in a clandestine fashion with a lover. It is as if they had brought with them the atmosphere of the parental home and transferred it to their marriage. These disturbed people have a habit of seeing their spouses in the same light as their parents, and consequently it is unthinkable to indulge in sex in their own house. Instead they creep out like guilty teenagers to a forbidden source of sexual indulgence.

The suffering caused by such behaviour, both to the disturbed person and their families (and this pattern occurs in both men and women) is of course enormous. By any standards it is to be deprecated. Yet is it rational on our part to deal with this sort of behaviour by moral condemnation? I think not. If I am right in believing that a sense of sexual guilt is important in motivating sexually deviant behaviour, then to respond in a way calculated to make the client more guilty can be expected to increase rather than decrease the chance of further offences. I am sure that our answer to guilt must concern itself in some way more with forgiveness rather than with castigation.

When psychiatrists talk about guilt they usually mean by this the emotional reactions or affects associated with guilt. These affects may be justifiable, such as the remorse that is felt after one has hurt a loved one in an angry outburst, or they may be morbid and irrational, as in the self-reproach which occurs in the depressive reaction following a bereavement. To the lawyer, however, and to some extent the theologian, guilt refers not to feelings but to fact—the fact of accountability on the part of a (sane) individual towards the acts he performs. It is not that psychiatrists are uninterested in accountability: indeed, a denial on the part of the patient of responsibility for his actions is a serious hindrance to treatment unless he is psychotic. The point I wish to make here is that feelings of guilt may easily become morbidly exaggerated even when there is some rational cause for them, and they then are a serious difficulty to effective action. Real and rational concern over the distress of someone whom one has injured can so easily turn into a self-centred sentiment in which the guilty person indulges in an orgy of self-reproach.

To my mind, true feelings of guilt are reasonable only as a response to the suffering of a person whom we have hurt or let down. Under these circumstances, reparation and remorse have real meaning. But more often we are judged guilty because we have transgressed a norm of behaviour set either by ourselves or by a social institution. We suffer because of the loss of self-esteem and fear that we may lose the respect and affection of others. These are self-regarding sentiments and, although natural in themselves, I am sure they are unhelpful, and should be discouraged.

I have said that loneliness is essentially the consequence of the breakdown of emotional transactions between people. We can now see the part played by guilt in this breakdown. When through our own actions we lose our own self-esteem and are in danger of losing the respect of others, we become angry with ourselves and tend to move away from people to avoid the expected rebuff. Sometimes the guilty person demands excessive reassurances from those around that he has not lost their love, and these irrational demands can be so irritating that they provoke the rebuff which he most fears. Either way, the guilty person becomes increasingly estranged from his fellows, and increasingly lonely.

On the other hand, a sincere concern for distress and upset which we cause in other people, and a willingness to accept responsibility for the consequences of our actions do more than anything to strengthen the bonds between ourselves and others.

Our answer to the various problems of man is in no sense a technique to be described in detail. Unless the despairing man believes that we can enter into his feeling of despair, only then can we help him find the answer, and how can we enter into his feeling of despair, until we understand its meaning?

The meaning of loneliness is, I repeat, the breakdown of the emotional dialogue between people. When we talk of providing an answer to man's problems, we are implying that the man in despair is already crying out, in a sort of silent shriek which passes unheard by others. If it only reaches our ears and we make some sort of fumbling reply by way of answer, then the dialogue of feeling will be restored, and the crisis of despair will have passed.

The simple offer of friendship is rarely sufficient, except for those people, like the aged and the homosexual, who find themselves in a physical, social isolation. But even in these cases, to some extent, and certainly in the rest, the isolation which is to be overcome is well defended. At this point, good intentions are not enough. How can the helper restore the dialogue of feeling unless he first senses the movement of feeling in the one who seeks help, and makes the appropriate response? Any other response is worse than useless. If you are torn by agonies of self-hate and unworthiness and you are met by the optimistic counsel to cheer up and count your blessings, then there can only be one conclusion: that the channel of communication is lost for ever and despair is intensified. Far from restoring the dialogue of feeling, an imperceptive reply opposes a monologue as answer to the cry for help.

Certainly skill and wisdom are required here. Skill to know when to talk and (more important) when to keep silent; skill to pick the words which will delicately hint at what has not yet been said; wisdom to know that the only solution to the client's problem is the one he creates himself. The helper's task is to restore the dialogue; the rest can be left to the client. The attempt to impose solutions is characteristic of the monologue, and therefore increases the isolation and despair of the client.

Technique in counselling is not a manipulation of the client's personality, but an expression of the type of relationship which is offered by the helper, and therefore, in the last analysis, an expression of the type of person the helper is. In the words of Martin Buber, "What do we expect when we are in despair and yet go to a man? Surely a presence by means of which we are told that nevertheless there is a meaning."

To restore the dialogue of feeling is to accept the person as he is. For a person to change, he must first be accepted as he is, unchanged. No change can take place while communications are broken. The helper must be able to accept the anger, the railings, the ingratitude, the guilt of the isolated person, if the sense of loneliness is to be overcome. Described in this way, I may seem to have cast the helper in a passive role, as if he were a sponge absorbing the badness which the client exposes. Certainly it often feels like this. But this does not really explain what happens, and indeed it often seems impossible to account for all that goes on between the client and helper. Perhaps it would be better to describe the helper not as a sponge but as a channel. I would like to end with the words of Tillich, who expresses this much better than I could do.

"In the communion of healing, for example, the psychoanalytic situation, the patient participates in the healing power of the helper by whom he is accepted although he feels himself unacceptable. The healer, in this relationship, does not stand for himself as an individual but represents the objective power of acceptance and self-affirmation. This objective power works through the healer in the patient. Of course, it must be embodied in a person who can realize guilt, who can judge, and who can accept in spite of the judgment. Acceptance by something which is less than personal could never overcome personal self-rejection. A wall to which I confess cannot forgive me. No self-acceptance is possible if one is not accepted in a person-to-person relation. But even if one is personally accepted, it needs a self-transcending courage to accept this acceptance, it needs the courage of confidence. For being accepted does not mean that guilt is denied. The healing helper who tried to convince his patient that he was not really guilty would do him a great disservice. He would prevent him from taking his guilt into his self-affirmation. He may help him to transform displaced, neurotic guilt feelings into genuine ones which are, so to speak, put in the right place, but he cannot tell him that there is no guilt in him. He accepts the patient into his communion without condemning anything and without covering up anything.

"Here, however, is the point where the religious 'Acceptance as being accepted' transcends medical healing. Religion asks for the ultimate source of the power which heals by accepting the unacceptable, it asks for God. The acceptance by God, his forgiving or justifying act, is the only and ultimate source of a courage to be which is able to take the anxiety of guilt and condemnation into itself. For the ultimate power of self-affirmation can only be the power of being itself. Everything less than this, one's own or anybody else's finite power of being cannot overcome the radical, infinite threat of non-being which is experienced in the despair of self-condemnation."

Befriending the lonely

Mary Bruce
Psychiatric Social Worker, London Samaritans

It has always seemed to me that the essential thing that
we in The Samaritans can offer is friendship. We are
dealing with people in despair who are tempted to
suicide, and I think there is a great danger that The
Samaritans might become just another casework agency
and so miss the very people whom we have set out to
help. I think that if it is made clear that we are helping
people who are in despair, who are suicidal, they will
come to us for help. They realize we are available to
them at that level. We must do all in our power to learn
about the different conditions from which they suffer,
and we must, where possible, refer people to the appropriate consultants; but we must not forget that underneath the presenting problem which the client brings
to us there is a deep sense of loneliness and isolation
which is, in most cases, the cause of suicide. Any amount
of psychotherapy, spiritual help, legal help, or other
help we can offer, is not really going to counteract this
unless the client is befriended. It should not be difficult
to understand this word 'befriending', but it does seem
to get misused a great deal within The Samaritans. Not
one of us can function properly without friends, and our
friendships are at different levels. I think we find it very
difficult to visualize our own little worlds without our
friends, but this is in most cases what people expect our
clients to do. They expect them to exist without friends,

and unless *we* are prepared to offer them friendship, it is possible that no one else is. Instead of just being an additional bit of help, befriending should be regarded as the main help, and unless we can understand this and can appreciate it to the full extent, we cannot offer true befriending. Quite often we are thinking of it as being second best, we are thinking, "Well, we can't get this person to a psychotherapist, we'll try befriending." But this attitude is not the right attitude. Befriending must be considered the most important thing.

One does not need training to be a friend. That is something that anyone who has offered to help The Samaritans should have the ability to be. But what one does need help in is understanding the different problems one may encounter in the people one is asked to befriend. In befriending we are not expected to go into the details of the clients' past or present problems and dig out information in order to make reports, but we are asked to be with the client in whatever situation he happens to be in, and at whatever level he is able to accept. In London, before arrangements are made for a client to be befriended, he or she is interviewed by a member of staff or by a senior volunteer, and considerable thought is given to the question, who will be the best person to befriend this particular client. It is not just a haphazard selection—so-and-so lives near, therefore they can do it—though distance is very important in London. Therefore it is essential that the directors and leaders and other people responsible for the interviewing should know their volunteers well, and should recognize their abilities and their limitations. It is also essential for the volunteers to have trust in their directors and their lieutenants, so that they can approach them if any difficulties should arise with the clients they are be-friending. There should be a good relationship between the befriender and the person in charge of the client.

The way in which befriending is introduced to the client is also very important. If the person interviewing really *believes* in befriending, this can be done very effectively. It should not be introduced as a polite brush-off or as a way of 'passing the buck', as in the case of one clergyman to whom I was talking about befriending, and who said to someone, "Well, I am rather busy now, would you mind if I introduced you to some people who live round the corner?" and was surprised when the befriending did not work out. The client felt rejected by the clergyman: that he was just being put off and given something that was not really of value. I think it is a good thing to be completely honest with the client and to tell him plainly that you feel his problems have got out of proportion or been made worse because he has been so lonely and had nobody to talk to and confide in, and that now you are going to see that this is put right, and that he will be helped to find a friend. Usually when one says that to the lonely client, he brightens up immediately, and then again just before the introduction is made he says, "Well, I don't see how you can do it because I've tried myself to make friends and it just doesn't work." One can then explain that in The Samaritans we have helpers who have joined us because they want to make friends with people, and can understand loneliness and isolation, and do become real friends. On the part of the befriender there is never a feeling of this being a duty imposed by somebody at the top, because he has joined simply in order to help people in the best way he can. If the director, or leader, considers that the volunteer can best help The Samaritans by befriending, as is the case with the vast majority of volunteers, this is what he does. The friendship that develops is a real relationship, not something that is just imposed, and there is no sense of being patronizing because that just does not happen. The friendships develop in the normal way of all friendships.

It can, of course, be a very costly business, this business of befriending, but it does not seem to me it is worth doing unless it is costly. If we are only going to be there at a level where we are not involved, it is not going to help anyone very much. It does mean giving up a lot of time, having people to your home, and doing all the sorts of things you do with your friends. And befrienders will always tell you that they enjoy these occasions, not because they feel smug because they are helping somebody who has not any friends, but because they accept the clients as their own friends. There cannot be any hard and fast rules about how often we see our friends. Usually we just fit it in when we can. But there are times when a client may be going through a great crisis and has to be seen quite a lot and given quite a lot of support. This may mean that a volunteer tends to be a bit swamped at one point. But the thing about The Samaritans is that we have always got other befrienders available to introduce. This can be done in a very easy, natural way, and it lessens the burden for the volunteer and also helps the client. The question, how long one goes on, also varies a great deal from client to client, but I think it is possible to make an assessment at the beginning as to how long this situation is going to go on. The people who are doing the initial interview should be able to see this, to see how long some situation is going to go on and to brief the person who is doing the befriending accordingly.

At this point I think it is as well to mention the hysterical personalities and psychopaths. They do come to The Samaritans, although they are not strictly people that we can help, and we have to recognize this in relation to befriending because they can waste a lot of valuable time. I think, if we can be aware of this before we ask someone to befriend an hysterical person who may have made an attempt at suicide, we can help them to deal with the situation in a better way. They tend to exploit in the people the very qualities which we like, and the befrienders find it difficult to get disentangled. I think we can help by seeing the situation before it becomes too involved.

The whole purpose of befriending is to get the client integrated into the community in some way. This is not an easy task because it is difficult to get groups who are interested in helping a socially isolated person, and after a time individual befriending is not necessarily the answer. It should be used to help people to become more confident and to try to make some new contacts on their own or develop new interests and therefore themselves to get a little more integrated than they had been. As I said, I do not think one needs any training to be a friend, but we must be very sure about the quality of the volunteers who are doing the befriending. It is essential for the befriender to be able to show love and compassion and to be with the client in his difficult situation.

Quite a lot of the volunteers who have these qualities have themselves been perhaps suicidal, or depressed, and can therefore understand the situation more easily. But it is not necessary to tell this to the client. They do not want to hear about others' problems at this point, and all that is necessary is to show that understanding by friendship. Befrienders too must be aware of their own difficulties: it is essential for all of us doing this kind of work to be aware of our particular difficulties, our particular limitations, and why we are trying to do this work.

I think we can help a great deal, for instance, with clients who are depressed. We would see that the depressed person was referred to a doctor and had whatever treatment was available, but I do not think that one can necessarily leave it there. A great deal can be done by befriending because quite often the depressed person has not got a family, has not got a friend to talk to. If the depressive who is going to hospital, each day or each week, feels that somebody cares whether he goes to hospital or not, this is very important, and a great deal has been done in London by the method of befriending to help people who have been depressed and who have been having treatment. Again, we have done a great deal in trying to help homosexuals by befriending, and accepting them into the community.

Befriending is accepting a person in spite of all his difficulties and problems: accepting him as a normal person, knowing that we all have problems. Quite often this is the first time a client has been accepted as a normal person. Counselling is not really enough; it is important, but befriending, this acceptance of the person, is the more important thing.

Befriending the sexually frustrated

Chad Varah
Founder of the Samaritans

The word 'frustration' in general is quite a neutral word: it simply means 'being prevented'. "I wanted to go and hear such-and-such a concert, but I was frustrated by the fact that my mother-in-law turned up and had to be entertained." Normally, however, when we think of frustration we think not merely of the fact of being prevented from doing or having something that we want, but also of the feelings which this prevention arouses in us: feelings of disappointment and usually, except in the most mature, of self-pity. Frustration is a difficult thing to bear because of these feelings which it arouses in us, and there are some who try to avoid these painful feelings by persuading themselves that they do not really want the thing which they are prevented from having. There is a certain amount of wisdom from the point of view of the preservation of one's equilibrium, in taking as one's hero the fox in Aesop's fable about the sour grapes. He could not reach them, so he decided that they were sour anyway and he did not want them. This is quite a prudent thing to do. But there are limits to the extent to which, if one cannot have what one wants, one can make up one's mind to want what one has. If there is something that we want which requires an effort to obtain it which is within our capacity, then the wise and mature person is the one who is prepared to make the effort, to make whatever sacrifice may be required, who knows what he wants and is prepared to pay the price, rather than to be deterred from wanting something sufficiently to go for it because it would really be too much trouble. One of our psychotherapists in the London Branch describes the neurotic as "one who is not prepared to pay the price". Such people go on interminably about the things they would like to have, and they also go on interminably about the things which it would be necessary to do in order to have them, and it is quite plain that they are not prepared to do these things that are necessary and yet they still go on saying they want them. In such a case one can doubt whether the person really ought to use the word 'want', when they mean little more than that they like to toy with the idea of having. 'Want', I think, is a very strong word, and ought to carry with it some implication of making some effort to satisfy the desire.

So then frustration is something which applies in life as a whole and not merely to our sexual needs. In Western civilization, which, however humanist or agnostic it may be in large sections, is still to some extent rooted in Christianity, we have never adopted in any general or widespread way the Eastern, particularly Buddhist, philosophies of trying to purge oneself of all desires. To try to make oneself a person who, not being an angel without body parts or passions, is nevertheless trying to live as though he were, is unchristian (for puritanism is a heresy). Regarding desire as the source of all misery and determining to be liberated from it, to want less and less until eventually you want nothing, not even to exist yourself as a separate entity but to be extinguished as an individual by merging like a drop in the ocean into Nirvana, does not make any appeal in the West, except of course to a few unusual individuals. The whole tendency of the Christian philosophy has been that right though it is to let the spirit be the master, not controlled by the instincts but rather controlling them, nevertheless the instincts are in themselves good, and the Christian should want a full and rich life. He should want everything that is going, not of course at the expense of harming or depriving other people, but nevertheless wanting it because "God has given us all things richly to enjoy". He regards fasting, for instance, not as an end in itself but simply as the occasional assertion in answer to the question, "Who is master inside my house, the spirit or the body?" It is interesting to notice that the Christian calendar provides only one day out of seven for fasting and six for enjoyment, and in the year only a period of forty days for praising God by abstaining from right things, and the other days, much more numerous, for praising Him by enjoying them and giving thanks for them. So then it would not be in accordance with the basic philosophy of most of our members, whether Christian, or agnostic within Western civilization, to be life-denying, or to preach any kind of puritanism. When, therefore, we find people frustrated in any realm of their experience our object is not to convince them that they are fortunate indeed to be frustrated, that they ought to learn to like this, and that the less they can have in the way of satisfactions the better, but rather to realize that frustration of one's desires, even if these are foolish desires or in some cases sinful desires, is a painful thing which can only suitably attract the compassion and the understanding of one's fellow beings. When a person who is frustrated (and I am still talking about frustration in general) encounters in the Samaritan ungrudging sympathy for one who is suffering something painful, this makes the frustration very much easier to bear. It is simply adding to the griefs and burdens of troubled souls to imply that they ought not to want whatever it is that they do want. We must avoid the use of the word 'ought' in any sentence which is concerned with peoples' desires. There may be cases where one can say what people ought or ought not to *do*, although Samaritans are quite slow to lay down the law in this way, but nobody in their right senses could include the word 'ought' in a sentence which is about wanting. Whether you want or do not want is just a fact, and there is no more sense in saying to someone, "You ought not to want so and so" than to say, "You ought not to be a tall man or a short man or to have red eyes or green hair [or do I mean the other way round?] or prefer pop to Bach or Cambridge sausages to Oxford marmalade."

Turning from frustration in general to our particular subject, sexual frustration, I want first to deal with sex as an appetite. We are familiar with basic appetites of the body: the need for food, drink, sleep, clothing and shelter. If these needs are for any length of time frustrated the effect upon us is bad both physically and mentally. We find that our physical health suffers if we are deprived of sleep for long periods, or if we are left starving hungry for a long time, or if we are unable to quench our thirst. Not only does our physical health suffer if these appetites are denied for any length of time but our mental health suffers too. We find ourselves becoming obsessed by whatever it is that we are lacking. The thirsty man cannot really concentrate his mind on anything except his need for a drink; the hungry man, the starving man, cannot think of anything except his need for food. He tries to distract his mind with other thoughts and finds that it does not work for very long at a time. The mind keeps going back to the urgent needs of the body. There may be a situation in which for a while he gets, as we call it, 'past it', but then the need revives and unless it is attended to the person will die. This is doubtless why our Indian representative always quotes to us the saying of the wise man in his country, "To a starving man even God himself would hesitate to appear in any other guise than that of bread." "Man doth not live by bread alone", but only a fool supposes he can live without bread or that if he hasn't bread he can turn his mind to those other needs that he has, those deeper spiritual needs. It is only when peoples' basic physical needs are satisfied that they can really give attention to those things which lift the human being above the level of the higher animals. Incidentally may I warn you against interpreting any reference of mine to animals in pejorative terms. I do not denigrate the animal kingdom at all when I refer to it. The animals are in the fortunate situation of being unable to sin. They simply have to follow their instincts and they are at all times pleasing to God. They are in the unfortunate position of not being able to choose whether they do right or wrong, in not being able to love in the human sense, and therefore incapable of that union with God and one's fellows which Christians believe is the object of life here on earth. So when I talk about the animals or the beasts I am not at any time talking sneeringly, I am simply talking of species which are different from the human species and with which we have certain things in common and certain things which are not in common. It is a mistake if you are a human being to try to live as though you were merely an animal; it is a mistake to forget that you are an animal; it is a mistake to try to live as if you were an angel; it is a mistake to forget that there is something angelic or divine within each one, including the ones you might consider least likely. So the person who is suffering from lack of bread, or lack of water, or lack of sleep, should find his fellows giving these needs priority, for he not only suffers physically but also becomes obsessed with his need and is incapable of concentrating on other matters which they might consider 'prior' things. The happiest situation is when our basic needs are reasonably provided for. Those flowers of civilization which are the arts and the sciences, poetry, music, drama and religion, are only possible when division of labour and increasing technology have freed us from the necessity of spending our entire day grubbing for food and still going to our cave hungry at night. Only when we have a certain amount of leisure from merely keeping ourselves alive can we begin to live as human beings, and our many frustrated people are in the situation of the person who is merely trying to keep himself alive and not living to the full. Christ said, "I came that they might have life and have it more abundantly." Life is to be enriched, and we in

The Samaritans try not merely to keep people alive but to give them a reason to be glad to be alive. We shall not do that if we feel anything but the deepest compassion for their frustrations and their deprivations and their needs which are not satisfied.

Now amongst these needs, one which we take most seriously but which the world at large seems to consider something to be ashamed of—both those who look down their noses at it and those who flaunt it—there is sexual need. The sexual appetite differs from the appetites of hunger and thirst in one very important way: it does not kill you directly if it is not satisfied (it may kill you indirectly). The person who is deprived for a long time of food or drink may get into such a state mentally that he decides to kill himself, but it is much more likely that he will die of the physical consequence of deprivation. The body cannot for unlimited periods do without food or drink or sleep, but sex is an appetite which can be left unsatisfied for interminable periods without causing the death of the body. If death supervenes it is because the effect upon the mind has been such as to make the person believe that life is not worth living, and therefore he destroys himself. It not uncommonly happens that the real reason behind somebody's self-destruction has been sexual frustration, when it has appeared to other people, in whom he has not confided, to be something quite different. Where people have voluntarily chosen the way of celibacy, which is a perfectly legitimate thing to do if you think God has called you to that, it is just a medical fact that, although the organs tend to atrophy a little after a long time, no harm comes to the general health whatever.

It is not dangerous to the health to leave this particular appetite unsatisfied, speaking of it simply as a physical appetite and speaking of the general health of the body. Whatever conflicts or struggles the person may have if he has voluntarily chosen the way of redirection are his own business. What we must never do, of course, is to recommend this way to somebody who already has a sufficiently heavy burden to carry without our stupid unthinking words being added to it. Never in The Samaritans do we say to somebody who is frustrated, "Oh, you should sublimate." Apart from the fact that this is a misuse of a technical term, what is meant is something which is easier said than done. This diversion of sexual energies miscalled 'sublimating' is something all of us do to some extent, otherwise we would never get any work done at all. One can only admire the way in which so many people who are undernourished in their sexual life somehow convert the energy which is not employed in personal sexual relationships into great benefits for large numbers of people—almost as though they were sharing their love around amongst many people instead of devoting it to one person. Not that I am saying that if you devote it to one person this necessarily means that you cannot spread it around too. A loving family is meant to be not an inlooking or ingrowing thing but a centre radiating love outward and sharing its blessing with others. The point I am trying to get across is that if a person mentions this unsatisfied need and there is nothing that we can do about it, at least we can refrain from implying that he ought not to have it, or ought not to talk about it, or ought not to grumble about it. We can agree that this is a painful experience, and we can sympathize. You might think it is not much help just to say, "Yes, that is tough . . . Yes, indeed, I do agree that is very hard." Well, it may not be *much* help, but a little is better than nothing, and many of our clients have been somewhat comforted by the recognition that the cross they bear is heavy. At least they retire from the encounter with us with a certain amount of dignity instead of going away with the impression that we think they are making a great fuss about some quite small thing which perhaps it is sinful of them to experience in the first place. They go away feeling that their problem has been treated with the seriousness that it deserves and that they themselves have been recognized as people who quietly and unsung have been battling heroically in a very difficult field.

I do not want you to think of sex simply as an appetite of the body, but we shall get all airy-fairy if we do not begin there and realize that this is something which God has implanted in us—a need which serves a good many ends, one obvious one being the continuation of the species. Our bodies do not know this. Hardly ever does it happen that some man pays ardent court to some woman because he is determined to reproduce his species. Obviously children are lovely things to have, especially if you are married—it is more convenient and it occasions less adverse comment. I have five of them myself and I would not be without them, but I have never yet met a married man (this may only be because I do not know anybody who is a nineteenth baronet longing for an heir to be the twentieth baronet) whose uppermost thought as he contemplated the privileges which go with Holy Matrimony was "Now

I can reproduce the species." You do of course sometimes get people who married because they loved one
another, have been married for some time, and do not
happen to have been blessed with children, and then
they try very hard and seek professional advice about
anything that may be preventing this happening. That
is a different matter. They did not court and marry one
another in the first place, one hopes, in order to reproduce the species. They were simply diddled by
Nature, which wants to reproduce the species, into
gratifying appetites which Nature, another name for
God, had implanted in them.

There are some people who talk as though to take
pleasure in the gratification of the appetite of sex were
somehow reprehensible. It would be blasphemous not to
take pleasure in it, where God has devised something
so admirable, so delightful. Not to find it enjoyable
would lead one to suspect that if one arrives in Heaven
one would have some criticisms of that too. The enjoyable is meant to be enjoyed and if someone doesn't
enjoy that which is considered by the majority of normal
people to be enjoyable that is a sign not of great holiness
in them but of some defect, like that of the person who
cannot enjoy the music of Bach: he simply has some
defect either by being tone deaf or lacking in cultural
education or having poor taste or simply being incapable of really listening. There are certain things
which are regarded by all cultivated persons everywhere
as deeply enjoyable, and sexual experience, sexual
gratification, is quite undeniably one of these. Therefore
we are led into some very useful practices such as the
continuation of the race, building our nests, bringing

up our families and so forth, by this provision of something which we, to a greater or lesser extent, ardently desire. I say to a greater or lesser extent because the amount of sexual drive, the strength of this appetite or hunger, varies very considerably from individual to individual and even in the same individual from time to time. It tends to diminish with increasing age, I am sorry to have to tell you, and it also usually diminishes at times of being run down or ill: it is usually almost extinguished in times of severe depression. But however much it may vary from person to person or from time to time there is no normal human individual in whom it is completely lacking. It takes different forms in the male and in the female; the male being generally speaking spontaneously sexed and the female responsively sexed. This also leads to one being the obvious pursuer and the other being the pursuer only by means of running away not too fast and looking round to make sure that she is being followed. One of the things which we frequently have to do in helping our clients is to interpret the opposite sex to them because so many men blame their womenfolk, not for being unwomanly, but for being womanly, for being the way women are, the way God made women. Similarly women blame men sometimes for being men. If you expect a woman to be the same kind of person sexually as a man but just with a different shaped body, then you are expecting something which is a monstrosity and which rarely happens. And if you are expecting a man, you yourself being a woman, to be like a woman apart from being furnished with a penis, again you are expecting a monstrosity. Men and women differ from one another in their fundamental attitude to sex, in the spontaneity of their sex and in their general emotional make-up, as much as they do in their physical organs. Yet the difference between them is not so great as to defeat comprehension or to make communication and responding impossible, any more than the difference between their bodies makes you wonder whether they belong to the same species or not.

So although the sexual drive takes a very different form in men from that which it takes in women, and although it differs considerably from person to person, it is safe to assume that every person who comes to The Samaritans has some sexual need. Whether this sexual need is being severely frustrated, in which case that is the problem that has brought the person, whether he admits it in the first interview or not, or whether he is doing quite nicely in this respect, thank you, never forget that any human being you meet—even if he or she does not appear very attractive erotically to yourself —is a person who has needs which are not to be underestimated or considered unimportant. Now if you are thinking of the gratification of the need for pleasurable sensations in the body culminating in an orgasm, then you are thinking of something where the frustration need not be long continued. It is only when you begin to think of the sexual needs of a human being in broader terms than the needs of the animal body that you realize the components of the frustration which are more difficult to meet—namely the emotional components. So far as we know the animal simply wants the relief of the sexual tension which has been built up. In the case of the male animal this is by orgasm. The enjoyment of the female animal is somewhat different, though human females need orgasm too. When we turn to the human being there is a greater emotional need for a love relationship in both male and female than there is a physical need for an orgasm. This applies even more to the female than to the male, but it applies very much more to the male than is usually recognized. Quite a large proportion of those who come to us complaining of sexual frustration and whom we are unable to help in any direct way nevertheless do, after having been befriended and made to feel that somebody cares about them and thus released from this terrible obsession of only being able to think about the one need, experience what they call diminution of their sexual frustration. What happens of course is not that their sexual difficulties or their sexual needs diminish but that the emotional components which they were misinterpreting as physical hunger are dealt with and therefore the physical hunger is cut down to size and seen as the size it is. It may still be big and painful, but it will be less painful than when a great deal of emotional need was being mixed up with it and confused with it, or interpreted as sexual frustration in the narrower sense. The person who was sexually frustrated in the *broader* sense (both physically and emotionally) was assuming that it was only physical.

Now I say that our Samaritan befriending can, to some extent, make up for this emotional lack: only to some extent because, of course, as one of my clients so pathetically put it, when Adam was lonely God didn't create for him ten friends but one wife. This client was one who had reached the age of about sixty without ever having had a man desire her, and although she was given a great deal of Samaritan befriending and this did help and she was most grateful, it still did not meet her need to be of great importance in a very intimate way to one chosen person. She did manage to get a great deal of satisfaction by fixing her longings and desires on somebody whom in fact she did not know —I think she had seen him on one occasion speaking at a meeting on a platform, she being in the body of the hall, and she managed to persuade herself that he had noticed her and that there was some devious reason why he did not get into direct touch with her. There would have been no point in trying to discourage this fantasy which appeared to give her some satisfaction.

So then in dealing with clients with sexual frustration we have to realize that our befriending consists of two things: (1) recognizing it as a very painful thing, not minimizing it, not pretending that they ought not to suffer from it, and (2) dealing with the component of this frustration which we as Samaritans may deal with. We are not permitted to deal with the purely physical side of the need of the clients. We are not able (even by resigning from the organization) to enter into a personal relationship of the kind a person wants—marry them for instance—more than once. So the befriending we are able to give only deals with a fraction of the need; but half a loaf or a quarter of a loaf is better than no bread, and the other components of sexual frustration are very much easier to bear and to cope with if you have friends who sympathize and who do give you such affection as it is right for them to give. Even if you find cases where the client becomes so fond of you and is so grateful for your friendship that he or she longs for some erotic expression of this and is disappointed because it is not possible in the Samaritan relationship to engage in this at all, nevertheless his or her disappointment that you are unable to give expression to your affection in this particular way does not destroy the value of the friendship in the majority of cases. The client would rather have a friend of whom he or she would like more than can be given, than not have a friend. And to have someone who loves you and says, "No— sorry," is a less unhappy situation than to be alone and disregarded, surrounded by jostling strangers some of whom might well say "Yes" to this particular question but "No" to any genuine care or long-term concern.

As far as purely physical components of sexual frustration are concerned, these can in both sexes be dealt with otherwise than in the context of a love relationship of a mutual kind which is obviously the ideal. Of course, what any normal person wants—not that all our clients are normal—is a relationship of mutual love of which sex is part of the expression. But if we are thinking of the physical component, of the need of the appetite which we have compared with hunger and thirst, and if we are thinking of those who have not chosen either to deny this appetite or to divert their energies into other channels, there still is the possibility which of course most of our clients are aware of, of dealing with the purely physical side of their need by their own efforts in masturbation. In some cases they obtain gratification of their physical need with someone who does not love them—who indeed, if a prostitute, hates and despises them, or, if a frigid wife, is simply unresponsive and not very willing. In some cases they are able to obtain the satisfaction of the physical side of their need in a context which is quite unacceptable, e.g. where a homosexual is married, as many are, in some cases quite contentedly in many ways, the kind of physical relationship which he would like to have is not with women at all; nevertheless with a woman it does give, if he is able to have it, some relief. Similarly the case of the lesbian married to a heterosexual male. But whether by masturbation or by some form of sexual activity which is not really acceptable, not really what the person wants, or some kind of illicit relationship, you can see if you read the Kinsey Report (and its findings apply reasonably to Europe as well as to the United States) that there is no justification for supposing that sexual frustration in all of Western civilization is predominantly of this physical kind, because nearly everybody who experiences the urgent need of orgasm is able to procure one by some means or other even if they have not the kind of love relationship they want.

One of the things we are able to do in The Samaritans is to enable people not to think badly of themselves when they are driven to these various measures that I have mentioned in order to release an unbearable tension and allow them to be free of the obsession, allow them to get their minds on to something else for a change. I do not mean that we go around saying to our clients that they should masturbate more, simply because that is not the way to do it. The way to do it is to be very permissive and unsurprised and to take it as a matter of course when they mention, if they mention, if you are proved worthy to have it mentioned to you, the various ways in which they do make their difficult life a little less unbearable; and here Samaritan befriending comes in again. Several times I have noticed a case where a person has come to me for sexual counselling and was not apparently being very much comforted. Considerably *helped*, unless I flatter myself, by having certain things sorted out, but not really terribly comforted by the fact that I accepted the wretched fellow's visit once in three months to a prostitute, for which he despised himself, or his masturbation four times a week or whatever. He was not very comforted by the fact that *I* accepted this, and the reason seems to be because he said to himself, "This man is dealing with people's sexual problems from morning to night, nothing shocks him any more," and therefore my acceptance of him did not count—though such expertise as I have did, I hope, help him. But then he is given a befriender, and when he can eventually bring himself to speak a little about his situation and finds that his befriender, who is not an expert, who is not dealing with this subject morning, noon and night, accepts it in the same casual, matter of fact, understanding way, then he is comforted. Just as we often find that in matters of religion the testimony of a layman who is not paid to do it, so to speak, counts for so much more than the testimony of a parson in his clerical collar who may be believed to have an axe to grind, so in this matter the non-psychiatric or non-counselling person, namely the Samaritan befriender, who is not shocked or horrified and who just understands that people have their needs, and some are lucky in being able to gratify them in a socially and religiously acceptable way and some are unlucky that they cannot, can give much comfort; and instead of suffering from too great feelings of guilt or of anxiety, the client is able to accept himself as a person who in a difficult situation is doing the best he can, God knows. If you compare the total gratification that he has with that obtained by people no more meritorious than himself who just happen to be happily married, you can see he lives on a very thin, frugal ration, and to start begrudging him what little he does have would be unSamaritan in the extreme. The reason, in fact, why we seek to enable him so to conduct his life that he is able to form some sort of love relationships which may or may not include some sexuality is not because we want to get him out of his 'wicked practices' but because we know that the gratification he has found in whatever it is he has to do, is very poor compared with that which God meant him to have and which he could have in the context of the love relationship. It is not that we, like the general public, think of the people with their various deviations, perversions, counterfeits, substitutes, masturbation and whatnot as being a lot of reprehensible people who are having a wonderful time. We do not say, "Why should they have such a glorious, thrilling experience when we, who really behave ourselves most admirably, all things considered, don't have all this excitement?" but rather that here is an example of "To him that hath shall be given; from him that hath not shall be taken away even that which he hath" or another text, "Seek ye first the Kingdom of God and his righteousness, and all these things shall be added unto you." It seems so unfair that those who have found love should not only have the deepest need of the human being satisfied by finding love but should also get a hundred, a thousand times more out of their sex than those who have nothing but sex, either from a professional or from themselves or in some context which is not satisfying to them. When they feel that we are not wanting to spoil what little satisfaction or ease they are able to find for themselves, but are ambitious for them to find something better than they have previously been able to find, then they are ready to accept our help. I would not blame anybody at all for refusing to touch with a barge-pole somebody who wanted to cramp his style and spoil his fun. Too many people who have high moral standards, high ideals, do seem to give the impression of wanting to find out what other people are doing and to tell them it is wicked. When clients realize that our concern is that they should live life to the full, that they should have the opportunity to gratify their sexual needs in the wider sense of their need for love, for mutual love and not a mere passing physical spasm, then they take some notice of what we say.

But it is not so much what we say that counts: it is our whole attitude. And if they sense that we are sorry, that we are compassionate, that we accept them, that we wish them very well, and that we want to give them what we can of our own love, then we shall really be doing a good job of Samaritan befriending in cases of sexual frustration.

Befriending those suffering from guilt

Paul de Berker

Hon. Psychological Consultant to the London Samaritans

Guilt is an accompaniment of our everyday life, an essential ingredient of civilized living. As children, especially in Western society, we are subjected to a prolonged course of guilt induction: "Thou shalt not do this, that and the other, and if you do it you are naughty, you might get punished, and certainly Mummy and Daddy won't love you as much as if you were a good child." And this is the essential condition of guilt: that someone is not loving you as much as if you had done something you should have done. The result is a feeling of alienation.

At a recent International Congress of Psychotherapy, Ronald Laing spoke of the divided self, and suggested that Western society uses guilt as a primary mechanism to split us up into little bits and each bit disapproves of the other. He introduced some jargon which is probably so well known that I need not explain it: he talked about the archaic super-ego guilt, that is the guilt of the small child within us for, in fact, being as we are, whatever we are, which is working at the heart of ourselves the whole time and making us feel less than a person, less than a whole. He said that, in his opinion, with the vast majority of people, and all who come to consult him, and also from what he had deduced from his study of ordinary literature and writings of the West, this process of alienation is one of the most extreme pathological processes at work today. He did not offer any panacea for remedying it, because if it is an extreme process which is at work every day everywhere, to remedy it is an enormous task. But he went on—and I agree with him here—to differentiate between what is called 'rational guilt' and what might be called 'irrational guilt'. If you know you are doing something you should not do, and yet continue to do it, you might have some rational guilt. This is easy to deal with: one can say "I am sorry". But it strikes me that in most of the people who call upon The Samaritans—and, again, in ourselves—there is an enormous core of irrational guilt. I experienced this particularly strongly once while a student in Oxford just after the War. I did not like Oxford, I thought the people there a lot of silly so-and-soes who did not know what life was about. I was a sort of anti-teenage rebel, having knocked about in the Army for six and a half years, and I had some pretty hard feelings about my College. These were crystallized for me in an incident that occurred there. One morning the Dean called us together and said that someone had taken the sword which used to hang just above the High Table and had broken up the lectern with it. I knew I had not done this, but I had a sort of dream thought that I might have done, and this worried me terribly. I had not done it but my hard feelings had been displaced and would have found some sort of gratification if I *had* done it, and I wondered if in some curious way I had done it. Guilt had become attached to something which had nothing to do with where I started from. My own guilt about my own aggression towards Oxford and all it stood for manifested the possibility that I might have done this thing. This worried me for a long time.

I can give even more pathological illustrations about what I call irrational guilt if I introduce the concept of the unconscious (not that I need to introduce it, but to use it), where in fact any relevance to the incidents or circumstances which give rise to guilty feelings have long been forgotten in childhood, and all the patient knows is that he is tormented by guilt and needs to do something about it, to fix on one incident so that he can do something about it. I am again reminded of the client of The Samaritans a long time ago who was worried that she had said, "Damn the Holy Ghost." There is some rather confused text in the Bible somewhere which says that this is a sin you cannot be forgiven for. She said, "I have committed the ultimate sin; there is nothing I can do and I am condemned to go on feeling guilty the whole time." Of course I do not know what the theological explanation of this text might be, but it is obviously not something for which one is irrevocably damned if one says in transit, "Damn the Holy Ghost." But she had this need to fix her guilt, which was deep and hidden from her, on to some incident and then worry interminably about this particular incident and say, "There is nothing I can do about it," and it took a long time before we could travel backwards and find the context in which the true guilt situation was embedded.

Quite recently I saw another patient (not a client of The Samaritans, but let me disguise the circumstances slightly) who happens to be the Warden of a Home concerned with teenage girls. She had taken the girls out, and one had come back with a bite on the back of her neck. My patient said that obviously the girl had been up to some sort of love-making and someone had bitten her, this was dreadful and she would punish the girl very severely, and she felt very anxious about the girl's moral danger. Now in reality I suppose there was some modicum of danger which surrounded the girl, but, in fact, the amount of emotion the Warden attached to this incident was wildly out of proportion and related to her own sexual problems and difficulties with guilt which surrounded her, and she, in fact, was working in a context, looking after young people, where she had many chances to work out on them her own particular problems in this area. I think this was a great pity but it does happen and is something we all have to be alert for, in so far as that we may choose a vocation which gives us a chance to work out our own particular guilt problems, sometimes in a constructive way but sometimes in a way which I have indicated, which may not be so constructive for the people who happen to be within our power or path.

Now I suppose when one speaks of guilt it would be incomplete not to make some reference to crime and punishment, because we have a civil apparatus and the Courts which judge people's guilt, and they judge it always as if it were rational and conscious guilt. As you know, there is a category of people who are not quite responsible, where there is a diminished responsibility for their crime. After his own experience of English and Continental prisons, Arthur Koestler, in one of his earlier books, said that in English prisons all the prisoners felt innocent and the staff felt guilty, and in Continental prisons, particularly Russian prisons, all the staff felt innocent and the prisoners felt guilty. I do not know what we can deduce from that, save to say that perhaps what appears to be a guilty action tried before our Courts and often judged to be consciously and rationally guilty, may in many cases turn out to be something which the criminal feels to be perfectly justifiable and quite rational and not guilty about at all. Now this is a reversal of what I have been saying so far, namely that what we, as rational and conscious people, might sometimes consider to be worthy of guilt may, in the eye or mind of the person who has done whatever he has done, not be worthy of guilt at all, and may be quite a rational, sensible and straightforward thing to have done. I think this is worth bearing in mind.

The theory of penal practice says that the criminal judged to be guilty shall then atone for his guilt by work, suffering and punishment, and at the end of that time he shall emerge as a purged man back into society, who in theory should accept him as someone who has worked off whatever damage he has done by the crime he committed. People often wonder why this formula— which is, I think, philosophically and theologically respectable—often does not seem to work in practice. Really this is a continuation of the point I was trying to make before, that in the first place the criminal may not feel particularly guilty, therefore his punishment is not seen by him as an atonement but as an imposition and an offence against him, and he therefore emerges not purged but bitter. Added to this, society does not on the whole feel that the man has atoned but somehow feels it is still entitled to hate and to penalize this man who at one point, with all the paraphernalia of the Courts, has been judged to be guilty and whom society has ostracized by sending off to a secluded place, namely a prison. So I think it is worth looking at this philosophical and theological formula about guilt and asking if it does really work in any one particular case, especially if you use external and rational approaches to it. If you try to look at it as it operates from an unconscious or irrational basis, you can in fact very often see people trying to work it out inside themselves; and in the case of the woman who said, "Damn the Holy Ghost," and who felt that she had thereby committed a sin for which there was no redemption, in fact her whole life was spent in attempting to redeem herself by punishing herself and by suffering, and this took place all inside of her of course, at an unconscious, non-rational level. The sort of way in which she did it was by breaking up things, quite literally smashing them up, things she happened to feel were valuable: throwing her cosmetics downstairs, breaking her furniture, tearing up her clothes, breaking her jewellery, damaging friendships, constantly letting people down, hurting them by being rude and aggressive; and by spending her time in acute anxiety to such an extent that she was a candidate for a mental hospital and from time to time had to retreat to it—this in its own way being, as it were, a further punishment for herself devised by herself.

There are many aspects of guilt and its origins which I have not touched upon, but I should like now to turn to the question, "What can The Samaritans do about it?—What can anyone do about it?" And what I am going to suggest is probably what anyone would do about anyone who is suffering in some sort of internal way.

You may have heard of the works of Carl Rogers, who is the leading exponent of an art called non-directive counselling: he said that before one can be effective as a counsellor one must have inside oneself some capacity for the unconditional acceptance of the client who stands before one. One must also have some belief that, given time and the right circumstances, this person has a sufficient capacity of good within them ultimately to solve or to make some adjustment to their own problems. And if one does not have these two requirements, then no matter what one might do it will be of little avail. I think that Rogers states thus the two really main truths of any approach to helping people. But I also think that these are severe requirements to lay upon any Samaritan or psychotherapist, and so I will add a third truth. I would say that it is in every case almost impossible to meet these requirements one hundred per cent and in some cases one can hardly begin to meet them at all, but we as individuals vary tremendously in our capacity to deal with other people as individuals. Some people deal with some sorts much better than with others; therefore in any training and self-examination, one should try to work out some conclusions about the sort of people one can best tolerate and deal with, and the sort of people who one feels arouse such difficult feelings that one cannot really fulfil Rogers' requirements with respect to them. This requires a great deal of self-honesty and a certain amount of experience; when one first starts one feels guilty if one cannot deal with everybody that turns up: one feels lacking and inefficient; but as one goes on I think that with luck and careful and honest examination of what one does, one can say, "Well, I can deal with people that maltreat their children, it does not upset me too much, I can tolerate that; but on the other hand I cannot deal with sexual impotence (or something of that order). I can deal with homosexuals, but find lesbians very trying" and really accept one's limitations within the sort of formula that Rogers has offered. Now if one does that, and if one really does believe that the person has some capacity within himself to heal himself to some extent, given time and the appropriate circumstances, then I think one should resist the temptation to devise little formulae for one's clients, especially with respect to guilt.

The hardest task of all, therefore, is in effect to do nothing active but to remain receptive within one's capacity, always knowing where one's capacity ends; to be non-judgmental in so far that one in fact is not judgmental, and really to believe, if one can or in so far as one can, that the client has real capacity (given the right circumstances) to heal himself.

I think that is all the framework I would offer.

Psychological problems

Dr. Doris Odlum
Hon. Psychiatric Consultant to The Samaritans

We all have difficulty at times in knowing the kind of people we are dealing with and what really their basic personality and mental state is. It is in the case of people whose mental state is somewhat unstable that I think we find our greatest difficulty, because obviously the Samaritans are not trained in the diagnosis of mental disorder of any form, and the milder forms are peculiarly difficult sometimes to diagnose so that Samaritans know what they are handling. Obviously I am not suggesting that they can hope to do anything very skilled in the way of diagnosis, but at least they can learn enough to *know* when they are dealing with something which does represent a problem that they, in fact, cannot deal with. When to let go or when to pass on is, I think, a thing that requires great wisdom and experience, and, I would say, sometimes a good deal of courage and modesty. It is awfully easy to feel that one does not want to be beaten by a case. I often have to tell my social workers and my junior psychiatrists that they must not feel this way at all; that it is not a shameful thing; that it is not something for which they should feel guilty; because there are cases that only the most expert people can hope to deal with and even they cannot deal with all of those. I mean that we too know that we are helpless in certain cases to do very much more than just comfort. We cannot hope to cure, we may not even be able to palliate to any great extent. And we have, of course, to accept this without feelings of guilt, without feelings of shame. I think it is very important for us all to learn this: to know where we get out, and where we are right in getting out. It does take a good deal of practice and, I would have said, humility and courage, especially with these people who are in some way mentally different from the rest of us.

Now the subjects of depression and some forms of psychopathic personality are dealt with elsewhere in this book, but the type of cases of what we call the psychotic degree, that is, the people who are suffering from a real form of mental illness which affects the whole balance of the mind, include other things than these. One is schizophrenia, a name with which I think everybody is familiar today; but schizophrenia is a complicated thing. It is not just one condition: it is a condition that has many forms and facets, and it is not, perhaps, easy to say exactly what are the hall-marks, characteristics of the schizophrenic person; or perhaps we should say the schizoid person, because there are many people who have the schizoid type of background who are not necessarily suffering from the illness which we call schizophrenia in a developed form. One of the hall-marks of these people is that as soon as one comes into contact with them, one has the feeling of a barrier; one has the feeling almost of their being in a vacuum, that somehow one cannot quite get through. One has a feeling of strangeness, of what I always call 'the dark vacuum' between oneself and them; that though they appear to be wanting one's help, though they come to one for help, there is always this feeling that somehow they are withdrawn from one and that one cannot quite get over to them. Now this is a sort of instinctive feeling that one has, but I think it is a true one, and whenever one has that in relation to anyone who is asking for help, I would accept it as probably meaning that there is this basis of schizoid attitude behind it. Now it is very important to realize this because it will affect, or should affect, one's approach to them very materially. It does mean that one will very soon find oneself out of one's depth with them: that they may appear to be co-operative, that they may appear to be wanting to take part in whatever assistance one is prepared to give them, and do their share, but the odds are that they will not be able to. The odds are that they will appear to accept what one says and what one does, and then one will find that nothing of the kind has happened, that they have not pursued it, they have not carried it out. They have not had the continuity of purpose or the sense of reality to carry out the course that one has perhaps agreed upon, and therefore one will find that one is not getting anywhere with them. I think it is very important to know this, otherwise one can get very distressed. One feels that one is failing, or that one does not know where one is, and I think one must not try to do too much where one feels this strange barrier. And not infrequently one will find, especially with the younger type of schizophrenic, that these people also have a great deal of hysteria. I am going to talk about hysteria later, but I must mention it here because the hysterical over-lay is very common in young schizophrenics and they may appear to be self-dramatizing. They may appear to be showing off, posing—and indeed they very often are because many schizophrenics do live in a world of dream of their own, in which they are, in fact, acting a role for their own benefit and that of an imaginary audience. Now sometimes this role is one which gives them great satisfaction—it does not give anybody else any satisfaction but it gives them some—and they are happy in it. But very often this role is one which to them is extremely frightening. They have the feeling that the world is against them, that they are pursued by enemies or that people are not appreciating them, and they can become very hostile, and as we know, one of the characteristics of schizophrenia is a sudden impulse, so that they may do very impulsive and unexpected things. So one has always to be on one's guard when meeting anybody with whom one has this kind of feeling of strangeness or remoteness or that they are not quite in touch with reality.

A type which is very closely allied to schizophrenia is one that we meet very often in the world and that we call the paranoid. These are people who live in a world where they are suspicious, hostile, believing that everybody is an enemy or ready to be an enemy, very often believing that people think they are bad and very often, especially with women, that they are sexually bad. It is extraordinary how one gets women of a perfectly blameless life believing that the world thinks they are immoral, or that they have immoral ideas, and so one gets this attitude of hostility and resentment towards the world. They are very difficult to deal with. Not infrequently they want one to change the rest of the world to suit them—and this, of course, is not easy. At first one is the new thing, and we all know that with new people, like new drugs, patients are apt to make a rather wonderful improvement for a short time. It is very easy to say to oneself, 'Ah, you see, I have succeeded where everybody else has failed. This person has told me something which they have never told anybody else.' One gets a nasty shock later because one finds they have told *everybody* else. But for a time one might very easily be deceived into thinking that one has some white magic that nobody else has got. I had this when I was young. I had to be cured of it by some very bitter experiences. We all have it, of course. For the time being one is the only person who has understood them, the one person who is going to perform all the magic that is going to take away their fears and their hostility and make everything come right. Well, unfortunately this does not last. Familiarity definitely breeds contempt, and before very long one will join the ranks of the enemies. I think one must understand this, otherwise one might again become very depressed and distressed and feel that in some way one has failed. Well, one has not. One is just dealing with a type of personality in whom this is practically inevitable. It may be that they will still retain some slight affection and confidence in one, but one will certainly not fill the bill that they had hoped one would fill and I think one had better recognize that right at the start. It is often very difficult when one is faced with a person who appears to be so charming, so delightful, so attractive and who gradually, as the story unfolds, begins to tell one of their family who have never understood them, how their husband did not really appreciate them, how the children have failed them, their bosses have not done well by them. In fact, one begins to see that the whole world has failed them all along the line and then gradually it is borne in on one that they are the paranoid type. But one can easily be deceived into believing that their family has been very cruel to them and one can go around in a state of righteous indignation, make a lot of trouble, and make a fool of oneself, if one is not careful, as we have all done—I have done it myself, so I know quite well that one can do that.

These are the two main types which one is likely to have to deal with. One must not expect to be able to do very much for them, and must realize that it may be necessary to invoke the help of people more experienced and skilled in the situation than oneself. Of course, the difficulty will be that they are very unwilling to let one invoke help. One cannot go to a doctor, one cannot go to anybody, about a patient without their consent. This would be a breach of confidence. This is a thing we have all got to be awfully careful about. We must not do that, although we might feel (and we might be right) that it would be for their own good if we did. But still, this question of confidence, with Samaritans as with the doctor, is sacred. It is as sacred as the confessional, I always feel, and one should never, never break it. For although one might feel that good will come of it, in fact it never does. It always ends in trouble in the long run. So it may be that they will refuse to let one give them the help that one feels one could acquire for them by going to a doctor, going to a social worker, going to some agency or other. They will not consent and therefore one's hands are tied, and one feels, 'Well, what can I do?' and one cannot do very much. Even so, it may still be possible to befriend them up to a point, because these people are naturally very friendless and they are unable to make a relationship of love with others. This is one of the things they cannot do: they cannot love others. Therefore their own lives are very empty of love, and this they feel. They feel that everybody is rejecting them. The truth is that it is they who are doing the rejecting, but they do not see that, and therefore they are sometimes much helped by the fact that somebody does stick to them and is not put off too badly by their hostility and by the fact that they just do not co-operate. So sometimes one can befriend them when one cannot do anything else; but here again it may often be necessary to ask some senior person to give one some guidance.

Now we come to the group of people who are suffering from some kind of what we call neurosis. The essential difference between neurosis and psychosis is that the people with the neuroses have a good deal of insight, whereas the people with the psychoses, the schizophrenics and the paranoids, and those depressives who are suffering from the endogenous type of depression, have no insight at all. That is one of the characteristics of the illness. They cannot realize that they are ill; they cannot realize that it is they who are 'different' and they feel that it is everything else that is different. But the neurotics are very much aware of their differences. It is one of the things that distress them so much. They feel they are different from the rest of the world. When I worked in a general hospital—one of the hospitals of the Royal Free Group among others—I was seeing people who were not mentally ill, but who were emotionally disturbed, predominantly, and we found that about seventy-five per cent of our patients were suffering from some sort of anxiety state. This is the commonest form of neurosis that one gets. There are between thirty and forty per cent of the ordinary population who are in some ways rather more vulnerable and rather more sensitive than the remaining sixty per cent. These people seem to be more vulnerable to life in every way: they are more aware of themselves, more self-conscious; they are more conscious of the effects of other people upon them; they are more inclined to get worried and anxious and to find life difficult, than the other sixty per cent, whom we might call the tough. And they are a type who are very unwelcome to the other sixty per cent. The tough just do not understand them: they cannot see why they are like this, and they are often very impatient, and hostile, and even unkind to them. These more vulnerable types are largely people who are what one would call 'anxiety-prone'. They are a very fine type as a rule; the majority of them are a very good type indeed. They are the salt of the earth; they are carrying the burden of the community; they are highly con-scientious; they include the perfectionists, the self-drivers, who not only drive themselves but everybody else incidentally; and they are people who cannot tolerate anything below the standards they themselves have set up for themselves and for others. One can see that if one gets this attitude, the stage is set for a great deal of difficulty in the world, because if one is always feeling the need to be on one's toes, to do that little bit more, and one dare not sit back and take things easy, one is set for a good deal of trouble. These people, although they can love very deeply and frequently do, and are very good parents, very good at their work—very good in every way—are often people who are touchy and difficult to live with. So we get a certain amount of them because they are rather at odds with their environment and their personal relationships are very often upset. Samaritans do get quite a number of these coming to them, I know, for one reason or another. Very often it is their husbands or wives that they cannot get on with, or their children, especially their adolescent children, or it is their jobs they cannot get on with, a boss or a colleague upsets them. A certain feeling of tension, of apprehension, is their hall-mark. One can see it the moment a person of that type comes into the room. One can tell that they are that type, and one knows that one is going to have difficulty in helping them just because they are going to find it frightfully difficult to change in any way this rigid standard and attitude that they have set up for themselves. They are worriers, and they feel that they *ought* to worry; they feel that it would be in some way wrong and even dangerous not to worry. They feel that they dare not and should not relax. They have a quite unreasonable feeling of responsibility for what is happening, and they very often feel that nobody can do it as well as themselves. They are essentially the do-it-yourself type. And they very often overdo it: they cannot delegate, they cannot share with others. This makes it harder for themselves and, of course, it makes it rather hard for others too. A Samaritan will often get a husband coming and saying, "Oh, my wife, she never stops cleaning the house. I can't get her to stop. She is always doing entirely unnecessary things, and when I ask her not to do so much or to have more help, or something or the other, she always says, 'Oh, you don't understand, nobody can do it the proper way','' and so she wears herself out, and then she is irritable and troublesome and disagreeable, and here one gets a bad picture which can lead to a very unhappy family relationship, and a very broken home in some cases. So these too are people that a Samaritan has to understand.

They, of course, are not people that want jollying along. They are not people who want scolding, either. Both methods will have been tried on them by a good many other people, but they are not successful. I think it is by making them realize that one does understand how they feel, and that one appreciates their very fine qualities, and by trying to coax them into taking a less tense, a less rigid, a less perfectionist attitude, that one can help them most. It is not easy, but I think one can do an awful lot with these people; I think one really can help them, and I think one can very often help their families too, by understanding what they are in their situation. Now, it is perhaps a little off the Samaritan beat to mention that these are the type of people who produce all kinds of functional physical conditions which we call psychosomatic: the sort that is very often affecting their digestion. (It is, of course, quite common for anxiety and tension to affect the digestive tracts.) Such people get headaches; they very often get some kind of skin rash when they are upset; if they have got a tendency to asthma, they will get an attack of asthma. There are a thousand and one ways in which this anxiety type express their anxiety through their bodies. They seem to have a peculiar *rapport* between their minds and their bodies, which makes the body respond very quickly to any kind of emotional distress. And this is, of course, wholly unsatisfactory, because it only exaggerates their problems. It does not in any way alleviate or do away with the psychological problem: it just increases it, because they now have a physical problem to cope with as well, and the two reinforce each other. We, as doctors, I may say, find these people extremely difficult to assess and often extremely difficult to help. Samaritans do not have to do anything about the physical condition of such people, but some of the physical complaints which they suffer from are very strongly related to emotional distress, to a constant state of tension and anxiety. I may just say, *en passant*, that one has to be terribly careful as a doctor not to play on this string too hard because one can, if one is not very careful, assume that everything a patient of this type is suffering from is of psychological origin or psychologically increased, and one might be on a false and dangerous scent. But this is more a doctor's problem than a Samaritan's—although these people will often come to a Samaritan saying that their doctors are unsympathetic and do not understand them, and that they have all sorts of complaints which the doctors pooh-pooh and more or less disregard and just treat with sedatives or palliatives and never get really down to the problem. Unfortunately, the general practitioner today has never been trained in handling people and their problems. The rapid increase in medical science in the last fifty years has made it almost inevitable that the years of training should be entirely devoted to increases in scientific knowledge, and our real approach to our patients as people has been neglected. Now there is a very strong feeling abroad that this is wrong, and we are trying to remedy it. The medical schools are thinking very seriously about this problem and it is to be hoped that in twenty or thirty years' time, I am afraid not much before that, the general practitioner will have a rather different approach to people. But in the meantime Samaritans are going to have a lot of people come to them, who say that they are getting no help from their doctors. There was a series on the B.B.C. a few years ago with a Brains Trust at the end, of which I was a member, and we had thousands of letters from people, of whom more than fifty per cent said they got no help at all from their doctors. This was a very grave thing. But in the present state of our medical education I think it is inevitable. However, this is going to improve: it may not help the Samaritans very much, but it will their descendants, and patients of the future.

Another type that we get are much fewer but with a very high nuisance value, and therefore perhaps one is rather apt to think of them as the typical neurosis personalities: what we call the hysterics. Now hysteria is on the wane. It is relatively rare today, whereas anxiety states have gone up. In the First World War, when I was just coming into the picture of psychiatry, we had a large number of soldiers who developed hysterical symptoms and had to be invalided out of the forces because of it. We had very few people who developed anxiety states. In the Second World War, we had a complete reversal of this picture. We had extremely few people showing hysterical states, but we had a very high proportion showing severe anxiety. Now we ourselves do not quite know what has produced this extraordinary turn-over in the type of neurosis. It may be that today it is accepted that one can be frightened and nervous without losing face, whereas in the First World War one could not. The hero of the First World War was a man who never knew fear. And if you read the books of that period like Mason's *Four Feathers* and some other stories, you will find that the hero of that age was the completely fearless individual who never felt a tremor whatever happened. Today, of course, we would call him an insensitive fool. But it was not respectable to be anxious or to show fear, and consequently, when one was driven beyond the verge of one's capacity, one developed an hysterical symptom.

Hysterical symptoms are quite different from the psychosomatic ones I have been talking about, associated with anxiety. They affect quite different aspects of the body and the mind. They affect part of the body which is concerned with the voluntary muscles and with the special senses. And they affect it in such a way that they provide an escape route, by developing hysterical blindness or voicelessness or deafness or inability to walk or inability to do something else which at least lets one out. We did, as I say, have quite a lot of this in the First World War, and, of course, Hitler, who was in the army in the First World War, a conscript, developed hysterical blindness, was blind for nearly two years, and had to be invalided out on account of this. This was not at all an uncommon picture, and we psychiatrists were having to deal with it and try to understand it. Still, in those days, if you developed this sort of thing, you were very much out and you were lucky if you did not get shot for refusing to face battle. And it does seem as if certain personalities, even today, take this kind of way out. They are not the same type as the anxiety-prone. They are much more self-indulgent; they are much more self-dramatizing; they get out from under, as the Americans say, by this method, instead of facing up to it and fighting through it as anxiety people do. But in fact they are not such good personality types and they are much more difficult to deal with. An hysteric is simply not prepared to make the effort to co-operate, which, after all, is essential if one is going to get anywhere. As long as a patient comes demanding a magic, he is not going to get anywhere and neither is the Samaritan and this we have to realize. It is important to know the kind of person one is dealing with and what, in fact, they are demanding from one, what they are prepared to put into the situation with one's help or with the help of others.

There is also a type which I really perhaps should have referred to in association with the anxiety-prone, because they are very closely related to them and often one gets the two together: this is the obsessional type. People who are always chewing over whatever has happened. They cannot get away from it. Every problem assumes larger and larger proportions; whatever it is, they are always obsessed by it; they just cannot get it out of their minds. The obsessionals are difficult to help too because of this. This is their whole personality trend, towards keeping on and on and on with the thing and working it over and over again emotionally and not being able to get it out of their system. They talk it over with all and sundry and the more they talk about it the worse they are. On the other hand, they feel this compulsive desire to talk about it and to think about it and in some ways, I suppose, one can help them a little by listening, though I think it does not do them any good to keep going to different people and whipping themselves up emotionally about it. These are people with whom Samaritans can have quite some difficulty, but I think in some cases they can help them quite considerably.

These are the main types. Of course one gets people who are suffering from frank delusions and hallucinations, or who are excitable, manic. But these are not so common; they may come into one's office in a state of complete mental disturbance, as of course can happen from time to time, but they are obviously not cases that one can handle oneself at all. Why, though do they come to the Samaritans? Why do they not go to the hundred-and-one agencies that exist? We did research the other day in a committee of the B.M.A. of which I am a member, and found that there were twenty-four different groups who could go and visit somebody's house from the social work angle. So with all these groups available—there are over fifty groups in London alone, who can do some kind of social work—it really is rather surprising, is it not, that these people come to the Samaritans because they cannot find anyone else to go to. Now why can they not? Why do they not use any of these services which are available? And here, I think, one gets a clue to a common factor in the personality of practically all the people who come to one. This is that, in some way, they are afraid of, and a little hostile to, anything that they could regard as authority, because they feel they will be despised and thought rather foolish and inadequate if they go to them. I think the reason is that they will be treated as just a case and regarded as a cog in the machine; and, of course, there is unfortunately a certain element of truth in their fear, one must admit. This is where I feel that the Samaritans are playing such a wonderful role because they have none of the institutional stigma. They are not an organization in the same sense as the official organizations, and every person is a person to the Samaritans.

(This essay was first published in a different form by Delisle & Co., as a booklet entitled *Psychological Problems and Pastoral Care*.)

Befriending the anxious

Rev. Eric Reid
A Deputy Director, London Samaritans

Increasingly we have come to recognize the part played by anxiety in the causation of many of our common chronic physical diseases, now grouped as the psychosomatic disorders. When we consider the history of people who suffer from such illnesses, we commonly find that most of their lives they have been anxious people who have tended to worry about everything, and our attention is moved from the physical illness, a disease, to the particular personality in which it develops. Unfortunately the habitually anxious person seldom seeks help of a Samaritan, medical or spiritual kind before illness develops, and very often by this time it is extremely difficult to provide adequate or effective treatment to get him to stand permanently on his own feet again, and we in The Samaritans tend to become long term leaning posts, which we do not really mind doing, but which is basically not 'up our street', as we are mainly concerned with emergency and short-time work, getting people over hurdles so that they can manage the next one on their own initiative. I should, however, underestimate our problem if I confined it to that large number of people who consult the psychiatrist or physician, or local Samaritans on account of mental or physical breakdown.

Thousands of people today frequent the waiting-rooms of our G.P.s complaining of symptoms which are the expression of anxiety, and thousands more just put up with them. We are a long way yet from any reliable estimate of just how great a part anxiety plays in the development of physical illness, nor can we begin to estimate the unhappiness and wastage of creative energy which springs from the widespread tendency to worry and be anxious in those who never fall ill sufficiently seriously to consult a doctor or even The Samaritans. Clearly medicine alone can never touch more than the fringe of the problem created by the anxious, fearful person. Increasingly we in The Samaritans are coming to discover among our clients the underlying cause of anxiety which is so often hidden behind the self-confessed case history of the client in front of us.

Let us consider in general terms the nature of anxiety. It is something which affects every one of us, more or less. There are many things about which we all tend to become anxious, and perhaps one of the most common is our material security and that of our dependants. Many men have insured themselves beyond their means because they are so afraid of how their dependants will manage if anything should happen to them. We worry a great deal about money, the school bills, the overdraft, the mortgage on the home.

Another common source of anxiety is that connected with responsibilities. Many people worry constantly whether they are making the right decisions for themselves or for others, and feel an immense sense of relief when they can shift the responsibility on to somebody else. Others lie awake at night turning the next day's problems over in their minds. For some people, personal relationships are a great source of anxiety. Shy people are in a constant state of fear in relation to others, and many others worry about the impression they will make and what people will think of them. Personal relationships in marriage are a frequent source of anxiety. Husbands and wives worry about each other in many different ways. We become anxious about our children, their education, their careers, their manners and their morals. Lastly, a great deal of anxiety centres in the problems of disease and death, especially in those over middle age.

It is probably true to say that until modern times the cause of anxiety was largely projected into the environment; the greatest significance was given to external circumstances. This was understandable, since life in the past was full of sources of insecurity, and man was very much at the mercy of the elements and material want. In modern times, however, the picture has changed very considerably. Modern civilization has greatly reduced many of the external causes of anxiety. The Welfare State sees to it that nobody lacks the essential material needs of life, and the average expectation of life has risen enormously. We have near-full employment and good wages, and the conquest of the elements has greatly reduced the risks of travel by land, sea and air. In spite of all this there is no evidence that man is less prone to anxiety; indeed it sometimes seems that he is more anxious than ever before, and it all goes to show that anxiety arises not only, or indeed mainly, from external stress, but rather from conflict within the human soul.

Anxiety first arises within a relationship because the child feels his security is threatened. He depends for his security upon the assurance that he is loved and accepted, and he quickly finds that he has tendencies, such as sex, aggressiveness, dependence and independence which very often are not acceptable, and these are felt by the man to be bad. Here lies the challenge to us as Samaritans in the face of this problem of anxiety. What can we do during the course of our befriending of such clients as come to us?

First and foremost the Samaritan should understand the distinction between the salient features of fear and anxiety in a simple way. Fear is always caused by something definite, anxiety is vague. Fear is the tendency not to fight against the danger, but to escape through flight. Anxiety has a far more distinctive force, due to its indistinctness and haziness, for it knows no clearly recognized object and so creates tension and constriction. In anxiety one is in a state of being exposed to a situation with which one is unable to cope. The easiest way in which to exemplify this is to give a particular case history.

'Mr. A., aged 36, has been married for ten years and has one child of four years. Mr. A.'s father has been strict and rigid. He was the only boy in the family of five children, and the youngest child. His mother tended to over-compensate for the father's strict discipline. His father was an engineers' clerk and had been rather disappointed at his son's achievements. One grandparent died many years ago of T.B. The client, Mr. A., is an electrician and most conscientious in his work. At present he complains of "panic" attacks—

"tightness" in the chest and says "I cannot get my breath". He states that he worries because he is not very strong—in actual fact Mr. A. is six feet tall and very well built. He worries in case he may make a mistake when doing his work. "I may electrocute some child if I connect my wires wrongly." He complains that his wife is cold and uninterested in him and that his married life has not been complete for some time now. He shows a lack of affection for the child. Mr. A. always appears somewhat depressed, anxious and tense. He finds he is unable to concentrate for any length of time and is becoming more and more incapacitated as far as his electrician's work is concerned. He continues to worry about his physical health. "My grandfather had T.B. and my heart pounds at times." '

This client shows typical anxiety symptoms. He is a somewhat inadequate type of personality, and worries very easily. He has now transferred these worries on to his physical symptoms which are really only secondary to the anxiety state.

The Samaritan will find that in these states present day relationships are often very distorted. There are signs of an inhibited life due to anxiety and preoccupation with oneself. To one so afflicted the circle of friends will be small indeed, and interest in hobbies and other pleasurable activities lacking. The client will be investing most of his mental energy in himself, to the exclusion of friends and other interests.

The Samaritan befriender, under guidance from the person who is interviewing or counselling the client and working along with him, can help to take the client out of himself and turn him away from his unhealthy somatic preoccupation, and the patient befriender, always in consultation with the counsellor or interviewer, will very soon be talking with him, or, more important, allowing the client to talk to him and he, the befriender, grunting occasionally in the most suitable of places or even less occasionally in the most unsuitable of places. The client will, because of this concerned and compassionate relationship, be expressing his conflicts and his difficulties, and it is here that the Samaritan volunteer who is doing the befriending is making it so much easier for the counsellor in the interview sessions to get through to the client. As the Samaritan befriends the anxiety-ridden in this way, he begins to see where many of his problems lie and the point around which many of his difficulties centre: for example, insecurity over work, relationships with a superior, or unrecognized and severe conscious restrictions which he has placed upon himself. This kind of befriending of such problems will give the client much relief and the befriender can give positive support and encouragement towards leading a more full and rounded life. The client's relationship to the befriender will sometimes be coloured and distorted by the various difficulties and anxieties from which he suffers. He will constantly feel misunderstood by those around him and ultra-sensitive as a result of frequent rejections and defeats. Many will be extremely hesitant to relate and explain their problems while being interviewed or befriended. Others again will be excessively dependent. The befriender must handle the latter with the utmost stability and maturity, and see that not too much sapping of time and energy goes on. Patience, time and effort will be needed, and much will depend upon the relationship between the befriender and his client. One must not be perturbed by the setbacks which the client may experience, for these will occur until new reactions have replaced the old. Every step forward the client takes will be helped by the praise, support, patient concern, friendship and love of the Samaritan.

It is never helpful, though it is unfortunately frequently done by non-understanding people, to lecture, pointing out again and again the unreality of their anxieties. A common element in neurotic illness is a conflict which is in the unconscious and which, therefore, cannot be dealt with through 'reason'. Freud rightly said that one cannot fight a foe whom one does not see. The neurotic is in the rather helpless situation of only being able to observe certain manifestations of his sickness, without being able to deal with the forces which constitute the unconscious conflict.

In dealing with such clients, the befriender must realize that the client is ill. He must remember, too, that severe anxiety is often much more painful and intolerable than severe physical illness, and finally that the client is not consciously causing his own condition.

Many Samaritans are given clients to befriend who feel they have completely lost their faith, and that God has cast them out. They wring their hands and feel convinced there is no hope for them at all, as they have done so much that was wrong. They feel they are positively the most sinful of all creatures, and many will believe they have committed what in their interpretation is the 'unforgivable sin'. So many are in despair of having to live at all. Their eyes are red, their complexion pale and wan, and their foreheads wrinkled. Comfort is often fruitless.

The most important point for the counsellor and the befriender—and these two always work together—is the self-reproach of the sufferer. He has resurrected some false step in his past life and considers he is no longer worthy to live. This false step may be imaginary —probably invented to prove how wicked he is. In this state of morbid guilt it is virtually fruitless for the Samaritan even to refer to the Scriptures or indeed any other authority.

Despite their shyness and reserve, these clients look for someone who knows how to find a key to their soul. They are often deeply religious and their brooding brings them great spiritual distress and despair. There is here tremendous scope for the Samaritan to give comfort, encouragement and a sense of spiritual joy, and much will be done to uplift the client in the greatest affliction of all: utter despair and futility.

All that I have been saying concerns what is called misled anxiety—anxiety that has got out of proportion, the molehill being made the mountain— but there is an ordinary normal anxiety which is a good thing. If we did not have this within us—within our volunteers— we could make no progress with our clients. It is an anxiety that is creative, and if in our work within our own Samaritan branch we are not allowed to express this anxiety about our client—at such places as case conferences—then we will be inclined to go it alone, afraid that if it is expressed we will receive a rocket from the directorate and notice to quit. There is nothing worse in a Samaritan branch than the volunteer 'who goes it alone'. We are all members of a team working for the good of the client, and there is only one person who really matters within the organization: young, middle-aged or old Joe Soap, who is courageous enough to come to us and pour out his problem. Nothing else in our work really matters but him.

Depression (1)

Dr. Louis Rose
Hon. Psychiatric Consultant to the London Samaritans

There is in the depressed person a tendency to equate unworthiness and guilt with hopelessness, and either a desire for death, or a pseudo-intellectual awareness that death is deserved as a form of punishment. It is in this context that spiritual and religious attitudes may increase anxiety and depression, so that the desire for death may produce, in its own right, a sense of guilt when it is in conflict with spiritual principles.

It would seem useful here to draw some not too academic distinction between psychotic depression and neurotic depression in the sense I will define.

Psychotic depression is assessed not so much by the degree of unhappiness felt and exhibited by the sufferer but by the nature of the presenting problem as seen in conjunction with the long-term personality picture of the individual, if it is available. Most psychotic depressive symptom-pictures declare themselves. This means that the onset of depression in the absence of any, or of apparently adequate, cause in an otherwise fairly stable personality, belongs in one of the group of depressive illnesses which we call endogenous or reactive. Endogenous implies change of emotional state arising from within, and reactive surrounds a specific environmental situation recently past, or still present, which the individual is unable adequately to cope with. In endogenous depression the sufferer may seize upon a pseudo-factor on which to formulate the depressive illness. Perhaps I could here mention Mrs. A., a lady in her middle sixties who had tried to kill herself in a state of severe self-critical, agitated depression, feeling unworthy to live. She used to spend some of her time looking after people waiting for out-patient interviews at her local general hospital. One of her tasks was to make tea in the usual large urn, and her unworthiness was related to the fact that for the first time she had been a little late in arriving and had filled the urn with hot water from the tap, soon after which she had begun to feel self-critical and later severely depressed about having treated her poor patients in this way. The personal and family history was such as to indicate that this was a psychotic depressive illness, and she responded within two or three weeks to a course of electroplexy. By this time she was beginning to laugh about the incident and to wonder what the patients thought of the brew she had produced. This pseudo-factor was not the cause of her illness but merely the focus which every depressed patient needs for the emotional disturbance. Reactive depression, in which we include prolonged grief reactions, is despair of excessive degree for an excessive period related to a traumatic situation or event. For example, the widow who feels hopeless and lost, tearful and unhappy at the death of her husband, is reacting entirely normally to the traumatic situation. If, however, after a year or two she is still unkempt and the house is uncared for, she refuses to sell her husband's clothes or deal with his estate and loses general interest in herself, her normal social, spiritual and economic activities, this is a prolonged grief reaction which equates with reactive depression and since, as a rule, family and similar kindness and encouragement have not served, psychiatric help is usually necessary to help the sufferer to rehabilitate. Quite frequently this situation may be accompanied by declarations of poverty even though there are adequate financial resources, and this too must be recognized as part of the illness.

Neurotic depression, on the other hand, is most frequently met with in the type of personality which, throughout adult life and often earlier, has repeatedly exhibited or experienced inability to cope with the day-to-day stresses of social and economic life and a tendency to explode into a depressive state when each new apparently intolerable or even mildly unpleasant or unacceptable situation has arisen. Frequently the individual's own inadequacy in the context concerned is the basis of the depression. Sometimes the awareness of inadequacy and the crude fact of inferiority spreads throughout the whole of the individual's life pattern as a chronic depressive state—better or worse depending on the temporary situation; quite frequently it is reserved for the social, occupational or sexual sector of immediate existence, and the man who is depressed and withdrawn with women may be the life and soul of the party in the pub. Mr. B. had long-term marital and sexual difficulties, and had for some years been planning his death by accident, having not responded to a fair amount of auxiliary medical support. Within a few months some of the more obscure difficulties had been brought into consciousness, and he is now living a comparatively pleasant and satisfying life at all levels. But because the problem was one of neurotic depression it seems reasonable to be afraid that some new problem in the future, or the reappearance of some aspect of the old one, may precipitate mild depression again. Mr. C., a man in his forties, was suffering from depression. He was a professional man whose story was something like this. Employed by a Local Authority, he had sought to increase his income by gambling; he inevitably decreased it. He therefore tried to make up the difference by doing some work in his spare time, so that he became afraid that his employing authority might discover this and sack him; and as a corollary to this it was necessary for him to conceal from the income tax authorities his private earnings. Having made some extra money in this way, he then tried to recoup his losses by some more unsuccessful gambling, so the economic stress, self-criticism, fear of loss of employment and consequent disaster for his family and himself led to a state of incapacity which in general terms was a state of mild reactive depression. This man was, I thought, suffering from neurotic reaction related to his own incapacity to cope with the situation, and we did at long last get him to recognize that the simplest and most effective way of treating this disorder was to begin to live with the facts of life, stop losing money gambling, explain the situation to the income tax authorities, and, so far as I know, from that particular stage there has been considerable improvement in his self-discipline. This was not so much a case for psychotherapy as for counselling and support.

What is common to these various academically classified states is the sense of failure and the threat of dissolution, fear of deep unhappiness, and the desire to escape from it by suicide. Lack of experience may be responsible for helpers being afraid of discussing the will to suicide of depressed patients: the depressed patient is finding life difficult if not intolerable, and the suicidal content may vary from unspecified lack of desire to go on living to ideas of suicide, fear of an impulse to kill oneself, and in severe depressive states specifically working out how suicide can be achieved. It is necessary to find out which state of suicidal initiative has been reached in order to assess the type of management and treatment needed by the sufferer.

In the course of my first interview I usually ask patients if they have occasionally thought life not worth living, proceeding gradually to discover whether they have actually thought of suicide and if so of a method. (The ubiquitous pill has become a ready and insidiously comfortable weapon.) One need not fear that discussing suicide will cause a patient either to think of it for the first time or, having thought of it before, put it into practice—the neurotically depressed want help and the psychotically depressed do not care.

Suicide itself may be part of a cultural pattern in that there are communities in which it is socially acceptable and others in which it is spiritually and socially objectionable. It would be perhaps worth mentioning that there are fashions in suicide: one thinks of Plutarch's Maidens of Miletos, who were given to hanging themselves, until stopped by public edict that the bodies would be stripped and exhibited, of the not long past Chinese custom of protest by hanging, and of 'mihara yama', meaning, roughly, death rather than dishonour, in Japan. Some degree of hysteria must have contributed to 167 suicides in one year by jumping into a volcano crater in Japan. More recently, the *auto-da-fé* of Burmese monks has demonstrated a form of social protest of different psychodynamics. Studies of suicide in Scandinavia and elsewhere are relevant, but we are more concerned with the situations in which there is a danger of attempted suicide. Some of the most important works on this subject, since Durkheim's monograph, are the Maudsley monograph by Stengel, Cook and Kreeger, and studies by Batchelor and Napier, and Schmidt, O'Neal and Robins. Perhaps I might mention here that over the past months I have, with two young colleagues at the Hospital I serve, been concerned with assessment of the personality and psychiatric factors leading to admission following attempted suicide; the first part of this study will, I hope, be published soon. I am collaborating also with Dr. H. Lehmann of Cambridge in a biochemical study of depressed patients, which seems to be yielding significant figures. Others are carrying out research into the effect of changes in the electrolyte balance on mental states.

Many people who seek help from The Samaritans are suffering from one or other type of depressive state, and the fact of their doing so implies awareness of the temptation to kill themselves. They have been desperate enough to think of it, but perhaps fear it or lack the urgent death-wish or initiative: there may be a remnant of insight enabling them to realize that this is an emotional reaction which, if relieved, might enable them to cope with the problems surrounding them.

People whose insight enables them to reach out for help are in general more likely to be suffering from neurotic than psychotic depression, in the sense that there is, as I said, an inability to cope without help in an apparently intractable situation from which death seems a comparatively less unpleasant alternative, but although desperate they *hope* for help. The spiritual attitude, religious belief and ideas of after-life are here involved. The range of such problems cannot be touched in a brief comment such as this, but I have already mentioned some of the common factors which, without calling for any special knowledge of the psychodynamics, are obvious. As I have said, spiritual, sexual, economic and social difficulties occur frequently in the case history series, and it sometimes calls for very special experience to elucidate the features which are primary. Touching on two of these factors briefly, I would like to mention opinions based on two patient studies: one, which included the death of a pregnant woman, reached the conclusion that there are no psychiatric grounds for terminating pregnancy and—I speak from memory—the statement that pregnant women never kill themselves. In the other study about six per cent of the women who killed themselves while of childbearing age were pregnant. What is certain is that unwanted pregnancy may be responsible for a state of depression accompanied by ideas of suicide, and the prospective mother is in need of help at that time as a life-saving measure, support and treatment arranged accordingly. Only rarely the depressive reaction is sufficiently severe to warrant the consideration of advising termination of pregnancy. This is not the time or the place to define the criteria for such advice, but I would like to mention a lady referred to me recently. This patient had had one child a few years previously, after forty-eight hours of labour, with manual removal of the placenta followed by haemorrhage of about three pints. She had been severely disturbed by this experience and in spite of contraception she was again pregnant. She was terrified of the prospect of repetition of this severe mental and physical trauma but I thought her state was compatible with the circumstances as they seemed to her at the time. I did, however, think that with adequate support and reassurance over the months she could learn to adjust to the situation and that she might reasonably be expected to enjoy having another child rather than fear the birth of it.

Needs of this sort and the needs of people suffering from reactions to other situations have led to the significant contribution the Samaritans are making to society. It is, of course, necessary to have experienced, intelligent and wise (the latter two do not necessarily equate) people capable of recognizing when lay management in the care of volunteers is not adequate to the task. One of the important keys to this problem is the ability to recognize when the patient's reaction is inappropriate in type, rather than degree—as would be clear from the study of Mrs. A. contrasted with Mr. C. Referral for psychiatric assessment would obviously be best in all cases, but this is hardly practicable with the present patient/doctor availability ratio, so that wise and competent filtering is needed to separate those who need psychiatric help urgently from those who can benefit from Samaritan befriending and counselling.

One final point is the factor of initiative. The patient who is so depressed as to be unable to reach out for the nearest and simplest suicidal weapon will be safe for the time, but this lack of initiative may also prevent a call on the Samaritan service. It is when initiative returns that stray factors of family and social significance may, simply as a matter of luck, swing the patient towards a suicidal gesture or towards the telephone. Quite frequently there are no friends, family or doctor in the picture, and this is when the tragedies occur. But where there is somebody who is sufficiently aware of the patient's distress to give or arrange help, or encourage the patient to seek it, the function of The Samaritans begins to operate, the telephone being the usual way of making the first approach to more personal forms of help. Perhaps more significant is the patient's insight into the degree and nature of his or her despair, and the knowledge that there *is* a Samaritan dictates the action which may lead to mental and physical salvation.

Depression (2)

Dr. Richard Fox
Hon. Psychiatric Consultant to The Samaritans

Everybody, surely, has been depressed at one time or another: by bereavement, failing an examination, or just getting downright miserable for some quite trivial cause, or even for no cause at all. But there are times when depression can become serious enough to endanger a person's life, to impair his function in his work and home, and to cause admission for psychiatric treatment; and this approximately one per cent of the population experience at some time during life. Women have it, so far as admission statistics are concerned, about twice as often as men, and, of course, in the older age groups there is a progressively increasing risk of depressive illness. It reaches its peak at about the age of sixty-five. Some believe that there is no depression of this type, practically speaking, or that it is very rare, below the age of about twenty. Severe depression does occur, however, in adolescents and children, though it usually takes different forms—disturbances of conduct, for example, like pilfering, or apathy and withdrawal.

In the adult depressive, the central feature, the most common and constant feature, is sadness, gloom, unhappiness that is obvious the moment the patient walks in the room. You see it at a glance: the features droop, the posture tends to be hunched, the gait rather slow and shuffling, and misery oozes out of every corner. Not always, of course. The appearance may sometimes be more one of perplexity and bewilderment, of not really understanding quite what is going on, or of blankness, apathy, loss of all emotional feeling. And again, the element of anxiety or fear may be uppermost in the clinical picture. Everything tends to slow up, concentration slows, the thought processes become clogged and memory fails. Things that were previously easy become impossibly difficult, work piles up in the office and starts a vicious circle, because the less the depressive manages to get through the more miserable he becomes and the less he is able to cope with the situation. Nor can he cope with things at home: he feels a burden to the family, as, indeed, very often he is, and everything becomes a terrible trial.

With the slowing up of the thought processes there tends usually to be a slowing up of the bodily movements as well, and in its extreme form—the retarded depressive—the patient will in fact seize up completely, and be unable to move from his chair or his bed, to go to the lavatory or eat or do anything: he will not respond to speech. But this is intended only as an indication of how grave this condition can be in its extreme forms, which are rare nowadays, presumably because of the rapid response to electric shock therapy and drugs. In the old days it was more common, and the feeding problems which the severe depressive caused doubtless contributed to the very high death rate— about fifteen per cent of the depressives in mental hospitals around the turn of the century—now negligible, I suppose. Sometimes the retardation is not obvious: the condition may rather be agitation, particularly in older people. In agitated depression the old soul can find no rest and is constantly on the move, almost night and day; unable to sit down for more than a minute or two, even in front of the television. The retarded depressive is less of a suicidal risk because he is retarded; he does not have the initiative to take his life. When he is emerging from his depression, one has to look out. This is a hazard of treating severely depressed patients as out-patients: they may emerge from their retardation in circumstances which are not, perhaps, so safe for them as they would be in hospital.

Depression appears in various masked forms. One of the most common is severe hypochondriasis: the patient who projects his doubts and miseries and fears on to his internal organs and develops the unshakeable conviction that he has got cancer of something or other, or, more severe, that the bowels are blocked and that the brain is turned to stone; but these latter distances from reality are uncommon. The depressive may hide his symptoms behind difficulties in the life situation. He may be less prepared to own up to his depression than to the difficulties he is having with the neighbours, with the hire purchase and so forth. I think we must, as Samaritans, see many people with this difficulty, and we must try to see behind the symptom, behind the presenting complaint, to what the real problem is. But this is true not only of depressives. The patient or client may be complaining about his headaches or his landlord, but the real trouble may be related much more to his sexual difficulties, or the fact that he always quarrels with his employers.

In psychiatry it is important, if one is trying to get

any kind of understanding at all of the case that presents, to see a relation or a friend, somebody who knows the patient really well. Unless one can get a reasonable account of what Mr. Smith was like before his depression came on, and of what he is like at home, one has not begun to study the problem. One must know whether before he was a normal, well-adjusted chap who got on well with everybody and did a good job: "But every now and then it comes over him like this, you know how it is—year before last, and then ten years ago he had a nasty spell, went into hospital, and now it's coming over him again." This would be the picture of the depressive, because depressive illness is a thing, alas, which tends to recur. But one can promise, I think, as faithfully as one can promise anything in medicine, that the patient will recover from this attack, and one can be quite honest in assuring the relatives and the patient himself that this will pass, everything will be all right and he will emerge unchanged, with an undamaged personality and things will go on as before. Indeed, he may gain something from the experience. We cannot say this with schizophrenia, of course, in which some damage to the personality may occur. This is one reason why one must know what sort of man the patient was before the illness came on. It is also important to know what he is like at home, because it is characteristic of some depressives that they are able for a while to put on a very good 'front'. They do not want to let themselves down. They will say, yes, they've been a bit unhappy, but really it was not too bad: they'll make out, given a bit of time. And then one sees the patient's wife and she says that he has been terrible at home—restless, around the house all the time, cannot settle to anything. She heard him saying things like 'hopeless' and 'better off without me' and saw him fiddling with the gas taps in the kitchen. Clearly if one gets this sort of history then one thinks in terms of fairly rapid admission, whereas without it one might let the patient go home. So, I repeat, a history from a relative or friend is crucial.

Suicide is the most disastrous, common complication of depression. Some people might say that suicide is always the consequence of depression in so far as anybody must feel really miserable to take such a step, and this is where we enter into an embattled field, because it is difficult to get data on what people think before committing suicide. Going over coroners' reports it has been assessed that forty per cent or thereabouts of people who committed suicide did have some significant psychiatric disorder beforehand, but that is rather conjectural: many people consider it higher than that. The completely logical and coherent suicide which appears to be entirely consistent with reason and carried out in a clear, normal mental state, does seem to happen. A case was reported some years ago of a lady of eighty who planned her meagre resources to last precisely until her eightieth birthday—she allotted so much per month —and found she was still alive without anything left, and so quietly, deliberately, ended it all. The coroner said it was a unique case in his experience.

So, with any depressive, one of the questions uppermost in the doctor's mind is, does this man represent a suicidal risk? Is he a chap to be treated with supportive therapy and an anti-depressive drug and sent home after a little chat to his relations, or is he a chap who ought to be in hospital rather quickly? Once it is put to him that he will be better off in hospital and that things will settle down much more quickly, then he knows that help is at hand, he feels more secure, and it is uncommon for anything to happen. Maybe this is why the Samaritan organization so rarely experiences patients committing suicide once they have come in contact with it—they have the emotional support, and feel that help is at hand. Judging suicidal risk is not easy but must always be attempted. People are often reluctant to talk about suicide, but if questioned tactfully, many depressed patients are surprisingly ready to talk about their feelings concerning life and death. The Samaritans are at an advantage here in so far as they exist to help suicidal people. Their clients are likely to come, therefore, expecting to talk about suicide. So it is not difficult for a Samaritan to lead off more or less straight into this particular topic. But in the clinical field the patient comes up with depression and one has to break into the subject of suicide somehow, for example, by saying, "Well, you've been pretty miserable recently?" and then, "You sometimes get a bit desperate with this?" and then, "Have you sometimes got so desperate that you wonder if life is worth going on with?" If all the answers are "Yes", one must go on from there. Is this just a morbid fear that he might one day become suicidal, or a vague tiredness with life, or a wish to die without meaning to do anything about it, or, finally, an active suicidal drive? A clearly formulated plan with hoarded drugs, or with the gas oven, is ominous; vague ideas—"I haven't really thought how I'd do it"—are less so. Especially serious are threats offering no chance of rescue—jumping from buildings or in front of trains, hanging, shooting. The suicide gambles with life and death. Always watch how he loads the dice.

Another hazard should be mentioned: the depressive who becomes homicidal. Women after childbirth are at special risk of this, but the condition is happily rare— one in a thousand maybe, of depressive illness. Judging the homicidal depressive is not easy. Usually one has no chance—the deed is done before you first meet the patient. It is the nearest and dearest who are destroyed out of a delusional feeling, a projection of the patient's own grief on to the person. He imagines that this person has no hope, that he is extremely miserable, and that he is doing the person a service by bringing this terrible state of affairs to an early end. A suicidal attempt usually follows. Anyone who studies the small print in the newspapers will have read of "family of five found shot in country house", and so on. There are these terrible cases, and it is always, as it were, a nightmare that one is going to miss one.

Anyone concerned in this type of work must seek expert help for any client who is seriously depressed, particularly to a delusional degree, i.e. in which his beliefs about himself and the world have deviated substantially from what you and I and most people would regard as reality.

Depression (3)

Dr. W. Linford Rees
Hon. Psychiatric Consultant to the London Samaritans

There are two main types of depressive illness. One is a reaction to difficulties or problems, catastrophes or losses, and is called *reactive* depression. In this type there is very often considerable anxiety, which fluctuates a great deal, but the depression itself will often lift temporarily when the patient is in pleasant surroundings or doing something which he normally enjoys. The sleep difficulty here is mainly a difficulty in getting off to sleep, and patients tend to feel worse towards the end of the day, because anxiety is a very prominent part of the picture and characteristically tends to build up during the day with minor frustrations and worries of everyday life. The patient has a great deal of anxiety, either in the form of an anxiety state itself or of a depression with anxiety, which is usually much worse towards the end of the day. Loss of weight is not very marked in this type of depression, but it does fluctuate a great deal from time to time.

The other type of depression is usually more severe. This is called *endogenous*, because the main causes of the depression arise from within the person. It is believed that in this illness there is a predisposing hereditary factor: a biochemical disturbance within the body, in fact, which is responsible for the person's illness. This does not mean to say that it is not affected by environmental factors, but the onus is initially or predominantly determined by constitutional factors which interact with environmental difficulties to produce the illness. So one might get a person who has an upsetting experience or who undergoes some stress, and instead of developing a reactive depression like the one I have described, develops the fairly typical endogenous depression. In such a case the stress is only the trigger in the mechanism, setting off this condition to which the patient is predisposed. Such patients are characteristically much worse in the morning; they tend to wake up unduly early—3.30 or 4 a.m.—and to feel worse at this time, very depressed, very agitated, their mind full of painful, unhappy thoughts; the day looks terrible in front of them. Usually by the afternoon or the evening the depression lifts and then they are able to do things which they could not have done earlier in the day, such as reading a little or even writing a letter; but some patients who are very depressed remain so throughout the day. These endogenous forms of depression are often severe and may totally incapacitate the patient. They may be so severe that the patient is in a state of stupor, sitting motionless and paying little attention to what goes on around him, responding very little to environmental stimuli. These patients are extremely slowed-up or retarded; if one asks them to count up to ten, even a simple thing like this they can only do very slowly indeed. There is a serious loss of weight, they look very ill and pale, their posture is dejected and bent, their muscles generally tend to lack tone, and it is because of this lack of tone that one gets the typical picture of a depressed person with a long face, furrows clearly marked, dejected posture, and slow movements. Now there are many patients who do not clearly fall into the endogenous or reactive types which I have described, and in fact in many patients there are both the environmental factors and predisposing factors operating. I think in practice it is much more important to decide how severe the depression is, because it is on account of the degree of severity that one has to take decisions regarding treatment or management.

A useful guide to the severity of the depression is the capacity of a person to carry on his normal work and activity. If the depression prevents him from working, this means that it is moderately severe or very severe, and usually indicates the need of some active medical treatment. Perhaps I can briefly describe the medical forms of treatment and then discuss how the work of The Samaritans can help with these patients.

In recent years the treatment of depression has been greatly facilitated by the discovery of new drugs, which have only been available for the last five or six years. Prior to this the only drugs available were the amphetamine drugs, and these were of very little use in depression because they lifted the patient temporarily and then after an hour or two left him feeling very tired, irritable, and as depressed as before. These drugs were only of use to patients who had short periods of depression in the early part of the day; for others their use was very limited. The first drug which was found to be of significant value was one which was first used in the treatment of tuberculosis. This was a drug called Iproniazid. When used for treating tuberculosis it was observed that the patients tended to become over-active,

sometimes very restless, and occasionally mentally disturbed, and because of these side-effects, which were all
due to the stimulation of the central nervous system,
this drug had to be abandoned for the treatment of
tuberculosis. But its side-effect on the central nervous
system led psychiatrists—particularly Dr. Nathan Kline
—to use it in the treatment of depression. This was a
drug which was effective in normal people as well as
helping patients suffering from depression. When used
in an extended fashion it was found to have undesirable
and sometimes serious side-effects, and it has now been
dropped; but a number of new drugs with similar
chemical actions and equally effective, but with much
greater safety, have now replaced that particular type
of drug.

Another drug which has been found useful in
depression is one similar to tranquillizing drugs. (Tranquillizing drugs themselves are of little use in depression: they alleviate the anxiety slightly but do not have
much effect on the depression itself.) This drug, which
was discovered in Switzerland, was really forgotten
about for three years, when it was tried in cases of
depression and found to be particularly helpful, especially for endogenous depression. It is called Tofranil,
and there are a number of newer drugs in this series.
There are two main classes of drugs for treatment of
depression: one is the Tofranil type; and the other type,
like the one used for the treatment of tuberculosis, is the
Mono-Amine Oxidase Inhibitors, a group which is
quite valuable for the milder and reactive forms of
depression.

These drugs have helped in the management of

depressive illnesses, but for very severe depressive states none of the drugs is as effective as electro-convulsive therapy, which remains at the moment the best treatment for the very severe forms of depressive illness.

One very urgent matter is the question of suicidal risk in depressive illness—the illness which more than any other carries the risk of suicide. The risk will depend partly on the severity of the depression and partly on other factors too. It is, of course, much more likely in the very severe depressions, but it is important to remember that the risk of suicide may increase as the patient starts getting better—a very important practical point. In severe depression the wish to commit suicide might be there but the person might be so slowed up, so retarded, that he is unable to make the attempt; but as he starts improving and before he has improved sufficiently to get over this suicidal wish, he might be sufficiently active to make an attempt. So one should not relinquish one's observation just because a person starts getting better. When he has improved further the wish becomes less and eventually passes off completely.

The risk of suicide is usually associated with the intensity of suffering; it is often linked with feelings of unworthiness, self-depreciation and guilt. The patient feels that he is no good, that life offers nothing for him. Another important factor is social isolation: in elderly people living alone, with no relatives or friends, this has been found to be a very important factor in determining the incidence of suicidal attempts. The depressed person feels useless and unwanted, and even in depressions which are endogenous it is important for such a person to feel that people still like him and accept him, and any help or sympathy that he can get is really appreciated. This is even more marked in patients who have depressive illnesses which are reactions to environmental problems or inter-personal difficulties.

In dealing with a depressed patient there are certain principles which are helpful. When people are very depressed it is often better to get them to accept the fact that they are depressed and that this does carry a great deal of incapacity and that sometimes when the depression is severe it is much better for a patient to accept it for the time being, because if he struggles to do things which he is incapable of doing, this only makes him feel worse, more guilty, more frustrated, and more disappointed. So at some stages it is important to get patients to realize that the difficulties they are having are normal manifestations of depression and they can help themselves better not by making violent efforts to do more but by accepting the disability for the time being and waiting until an improvement takes place.

Depressive illnesses, fortunately, are usually self-limiting, and even if they go on for many months or years there is always a tendency for the illness to end spontaneously; but with treatment and help the illness can be shortened.

Another important point in the management of such patients is to be able to assess the importance of some of the things they say. They will often tell one, "I am depressed because I did this when I was a child," or speak of something they are feeling guilty about, or say that they are depressed because of their work, which they cannot do and find very difficult. Now these, in fact, may be symptoms of the depression: the things they think have brought it on may be just the effects of the illness rather than the cause. This is an important point and is sometimes not an easy one to disentangle. Similarly when they say it is their work, this may be the early effects of the illness, but they wrongly attribute their illness to it. It is important to be aware of these points because one may mislead the patient if one accepts his beliefs at their face value.

One can be friendly, show interest, and give support: all this is helpful in all types of depression, but sometimes one has to realize that in severe depressions this may not produce very much in the way of an improvement. Nevertheless it is still important and still appreciated by the patient and he will remember it with gratitude later. It is important not to urge him to pull himself together, particularly when he is severely depressed, because he cannot do anything about it at that stage. As he gets better he will automatically find it much easier to do things and the need for encouragement will not be so great; but it is an appropriate time for encouragement to return to normal activities. Bearing these principles in mind, befriending by Samaritans can provide invaluable help in one of the most distressing and incapacitating illnesses which afflict mankind.

LIST OF SAMARITAN BRANCHES
IN THE COMMONWEALTH
* Branches starred offer a 24-hour service
on their emergency number

UNITED KINGDOM

*ABERDEEN

The Aberdeen Telephone Samaritans,
47 Bon Accord Street,
Aberdeen.
Tel: Aberdeen 53000 (Emergency)
      Aberdeen 53990 (Office)

*BATH

The Samaritans,
Abbey Church House,
Bath, Somerset.
Tel: Bath 5353 (Emergency)
      Bath 60128 (Office)

*BEDFORD

The Bedford Samaritans
17a St. Andrew's Road,
Bedford.
Tel: Bedford 52200 (Emergency)
      Bedford 52317 (Office)

*BELFAST

The Samaritans,
67 Lisburn Road,
Belfast 9, Northern Ireland.
Tel: Belfast 24635 (Emergency)
      Belfast 24636 (Office)

*BEXHILL
AND
HASTINGS

The Samaritans (Bexhill and Hastings
Branch), Caravan Centre,
Cnr. Harley Shute Road and Bexhill
Road, St. Leonards, Sussex.
Tel: Hastings 666

*BIRMINGHAM

The Birmingham Samaritans,
St. Jude's School,
Hill Street, Birmingham 5.
Tel: Midland 2000 (Emergency)
      Midland 1411 (Office)

*BLACKPOOL   *Blackpool Telephone Samaritans,*
              53 Queen Street,
              Blackpool, Lancs.
              Tel: Blackpool 20000 (Emergency)
                   Blackpool 20375 (Office)

*BOLTON   *Bolton Samaritans,*
              St. George's Road Congregational
              Church, Bolton, Lancs.
              Tel: Bolton 21200 (Emergency)
                   Bolton 24394 (Office)

*BOURNEMOUTH *Bournemouth Samaritans,*
              1st Floor Carrington,
              Wootton Gardens,
              Bournemouth, Hants.
              Tel: Bournemouth 21999 (Emergency)
                   Bournemouth 28090 (Office)

BRADFORD   *The Samaritans,*
              68 Little Horton Lane,
              Bradford 5, Yorks.
              Tel: Bradford 28282 (Emergency)
                   Bradford 31162 (Office)

*BRISTOL   *The Bristol Samaritans,*
              8 St. Nicholas Street,
              Bristol 1.
              Tel: Bristol 28444 (Emergency)
                   Bristol 28422 (Office)

BULKINGTON   *The Samaritans,*
              St. James Vicarage,
              Bulkington,
              nr. Nuneaton.
              Tel: Bedworth 2666 (Emergency)
                   Bedworth 2396 (Office)

BURNLEY   *Burnley and District Telephone Samaritans,*
              25 St. James Row,
              Burnley, Lancs.
              Tel: Burnley 23000 (Emergency)
                   Burnley 23061 (Office)

P   225

*CAMBRIDGE *Cambridge Samaritans,*
35 Regent Terrace,
Cambridge.
Tel: Cambridge 54545 (Emergency)
Cambridge 56420 (Office)

CHELMSFORD *Chelmsford Samaritans,*
17 Cottage Place,
Chelmsford, Essex.
Tel: Chelmsford 58838 (Emergency)
Chelmsford 58733 (Office)

*CHELTENHAM *The Samaritans* (Cheltenham and
District Branch), Church House,
1 Crescent Terrace,
Cheltenham, Glos.
Tel: Cheltenham 55777 (Emergency)

*COLCHESTER *Colchester Samaritans,*
Markham's Buildings,
Vineyard Street,
Colchester, Essex.
Tel: Colchester 6789 (Emergency)
Colchester 6636 (Office)

COVENTRY *Coventry Samaritans,*
St. Mark's Church,
Stoney Stanton Road,
Coventry.
Tel: Coventry 22550 (Emergency)
Coventry 21540 (Office)

CREWE *The Samaritans* (South-East Cheshire),
Christ Church Vestry,
Crewe, Cheshire.
Tel: Crewe 2144 (Emergency)

*CROYDON *The Samaritans,*
2b Kidderminster Road,
West Croydon, Surrey.
Tel: Croydon 4545 (Emergency)
Municipal 2905 (Office)

*DERBY

The Derby Samaritans,
110 Burton Road,
Derby.
Tel: Derby 40000 (Emergency)
Derby 48993 (Office)

DONCASTER

The Samaritans,
60 Thorne Road,
Doncaster, Yorks.
Tel: Doncaster 3636 (Emergency)

*DUNDEE

The Dundee Telephone Samaritans,
10 King Street,
Dundee.
Tel: Dundee 26666 (Emergency)
Dundee 25678 (Office)

DUNFERMLINE

Telephone Samaritans,
103 High Street,
Dunfermline.
Tel: Dunfermline 22222 (Emergency)

EASTBOURNE

The Samaritans,
The Christ Church Club Rooms,
Hanover Road, Seaside,
Eastbourne, Sussex.
Tel: Eastbourne 9933 (Emergency)
Eastbourne 4884 (Office)

*EDINBURGH

Telephone Samaritans,
8 Frederick Street,
Edinburgh 2.
Tel: Caledonian 3333 (Emergency)
Caledonian 3334 (Office)

EXETER

The Samaritans of Exeter,
42 St. David's Hill,
Exeter, Devon.
Tel: Exeter 77755 (Emergency)
Exeter 77401 (Office)

*FOLKESTONE   *The Samaritans*,
1 Holmesdale Terrace,
Folkestone, Kent.
Tel: Folkestone 55000 (Emergency)
    Folkestone 52947 (Office)

*GLASGOW   *Telephone Samaritan Service*,
134 Holland Street,
Glasgow C.2.
Tel: City 4488 (Emergency)
    City 7922 (Office)

*GRIMSBY   *Telephone Samaritans* (Grimsby,
Cleethorpes and District Branch),
Central Hall Buildings,
Duncombe Street,
Grimsby, Lincs.
Tel: Grimsby 4455 (Emergency)

*GUERNSEY   *The Guernsey Samaritans*,
8 Smith Street,
Guernsey C.I.
Tel: Central 3030 (Emergency)

*GUILDFORD   *Telephone Samaritans*,
95 Woodbridge Road,
Guildford, Surrey.
Tel: Guildford 2345 (Emergency)
    Guildford 2346 (Office)

*HALIFAX   *The Halifax and District Samaritans*,
Warwick Chambers,
37 Southgate,
Halifax, Yorks.
Tel: Halifax 62020 (Emergency)
    Halifax 66655 (Office)

HARLOW   *The Harlow Samaritans*,
54 Ram Gorse,
Harlow, Essex.
Tel: Harlow 24244

*HARROW
   The Samaritans,
54a Marlborough Road,
Harrow.
Tel: Harrow 7777 (Emergency)
     Harrow 5079 (Office)

*HAVERING
   The Havering Samaritans,
69 Western Road,
Romford, Essex.
Tel: Romford 40000 (Emergency)
     Romford 49339 (Office)

*HULL
   Kingston-upon-Hull Samaritan Service,
23 Waltham Street,
Hull, Yorks.
Tel: Hull 23456

*IPSWICH
   The Samaritans,
9 Coytes Gardens,
Ipswich, Suffolk.
Tel: Ipswich 51000 (Emergency)
     Ipswich 58488 (Office)

*ISLE OF WIGHT
   The Samaritans,
The Island Samaritan Centre,
Holy Trinity Church Hall,
Ryde, Isle of Wight.
Tel: Ryde 2277 and Portsmouth 23432
     (Emergency)
    Bembridge 2630 (Office)

*JERSEY
   The Jersey Samaritans,
Universal House,
19a James Street,
St. Helier, Jersey C.I.
Tel: Central 30303 (Emergency)
     Central 33090 (Office)

*LEAMINGTON SPA
   The Samaritans,
Lillington Vicarage,
Leamington Spa, Warwickshire.
Tel: Leamington Spa 22022
     (Emergency)
    Leamington Spa 24674 (Office)

P*

LEATHERHEAD   *The Samaritans*,
45 Lower Fairfield Road,
Leatherhead, Surrey.
Tel: Leatherhead 5555 (Emergency)
     Leatherhead 5556 (Office)

LEEK   *Leek and District Samaritans*,
Congregational School Rooms,
Russell Street,
Leek, Staffs.
Tel: Leek 4100 (Emergency)

*LEICESTER   *The Samaritans of Leicester*,
244 London Road,
Leicester.
Tel: Leicester 75000 (Emergency)
     Leicester 75330 (Office)

*LIVERPOOL   *The Samaritans*,
Chapel Street, Pier Head,
Liverpool 3.
Tel: Maritime 1999 (Emergency)
     Maritime 2441 (Office)

*LONDON   *The Samaritans*,
St. Stephen's Church Crypt,
Walbrook, London E.C.4.
Tel: Mansion House 9000 (Emergency)
     Mansion House 2277 (Office)
(There are Befriending Groups
attached to this Branch at Hampstead
and Wimbledon)

*MANCHESTER   *Manchester and District Telephone
Samaritans*, St. Paul's Church,
New Cross, Manchester 4.
Tel: Blackfriars 9000 (Emergency)
     Blackfriars 5228 (Office)
(There is a Befriending Group
attached to this Branch at
Macclesfield)

NEWCASTLE

The Samaritans of Tyneside,
1a Clayton Street,
Newcastle-upon-Tyne 1.
Tel: Newcastle-upon-Tyne 27272
(Emergency)

NORTH
RIDING

North Riding Samaritans,
P.O. Box No. 10,
Northallerton, Yorks.
Tel: Northallerton 3030.

*NORWICH

The Samaritans,
19 St. Stephen's Square,
Norwich, Nor.71.E.
Tel: Norwich 28000 (Emergency)
Norwich 21161 (Office)

*NOTTINGHAM

Telephone Samaritans of Nottingham,
2a Standard Hill,
Nottingham.
Tel: Nottingham 45000 (Emergency)
Nottingham 46464 (Office)

*OXFORD

The Oxford Samaritans,
9 Ship Street,
Oxford.
Tel: Oxford 44044 (Emergency)
Oxford 44593 (Office)

*PORTSMOUTH

The Portsmouth Samaritans
460 Commercial Road,
Portsmouth, Hants.
Tel: Portsmouth 23432 (Emergency)
Portsmouth 23433 (Office)

*READING

The Samaritans of Reading,
St. Giles' Hall,
Southampton Street,
Reading, Berks.
Tel: Reading 54845 (Emergency)
Reading 54846 (Office)

*REIGATE/
REDHILL
East Surrey and North Sussex Samaritans,
Basement Flat, 5 St. Mary's Road,
Reigate, Surrey.
Tel: Reigate 48444 (Emergency)
　　　Reigate 48445 (Office)

*SALISBURY
The Samaritans,
St. Nicholas Hospital,
Salisbury, Wilts.
Tel: Salisbury 5522

*SCUNTHORPE
The North Lindsey Samaritans,
31 Dunstall Street,
Scunthorpe, Lincs.
Tel: Scunthorpe 5555 (Emergency)
　　　Scunthorpe 61580 (Office)

SHEFFIELD
Sheffield Telephone Samaritans,
The Samaritan Centre,
Rockingham Lane,
Sheffield 1.
Tel: Sheffield 22221

SHREWSBURY
The Samaritans in Shropshire,
17 Butcher Row,
Shrewsbury, Salop.
Tel: Shrewsbury 4488 (Emergency)
　　　Shrewsbury 52401 (Office)

SOUTHAMPTON
Telephone Samaritans,
Above Bar Church, Above Bar Street,
Southampton.
Tel: Southampton 25999 (Emergency)
　　　Southampton 24466 (Office)
(Correspondence to the Secretary,
80 Ash Tree Road,
Bitterne Park,
Southampton)

STAFFORD
Stafford Samaritans,
15 Tipping Street,
Stafford.
Tel: Stafford 2121 (Emergency)
　　　Stafford 4673 (Office)

*STOKE-ON-
TRENT

North Staffordshire Samaritans,
Hanley Parish Church,
Town Road, Hanley,
Stoke-on-Trent, Staffs.
Tel: Stoke-on-Trent 23500
(Correspondence to the Secretary,
Flat 7, Bell House
Ripon Road, Blurton,
Stoke-on-Trent, Staffs.)

*SWANSEA

The Samaritans,
St. Paul's Church,
Swansea, Glam.
Tel: Swansea 59595

*TORQUAY

The Torbay Samaritans,
Cary Avenue,
Babbacombe,
Torquay, Devon.
Tel: Torquay 37171 (Emergency)
    Torquay 38080 (Office)

*WEYBRIDGE

North West Surrey Samaritans,
20a Queen's Road,
Weybridge, Surrey.
Tel: Weybridge 44444 (Emergency)
    Weybridge 47622 (Office)

*WOLVER-
HAMPTON

Telephone Samaritans,
24 School Street,
Wolverhampton.
Tel: Wolverhampton 24515
                (Emergency)
    Wolverhampton 25938 (Office)

*WORCESTER

Worcester Samaritans,
St. John House,
34 The Tything,
Worcester.
Tel: Worcester 21121 (Emergency)
    Worcester 28961 (Office)

AUSTRALIA

(Branches affiliated to the 'Centre International d'Information des Services de Secours par Téléphone'. See p. 237.)

HONG KONG

HONG KONG
The Samaritans,
40 Nga Tsin Wai Road,
Kowloon,
Hong Kong.
Tel: 821967

INDIA

BOMBAY
Bombay Samaritans,
St. John's Church,
Coloba,
Bombay 6.
Tel: 401.31

NEW ZEALAND

AUCKLAND
Lifeline Samaritans,
Inter-Church Counselling Centre,
Auckland.

CHRISTCHURCH
Samaritan Life Line,
The Dean's Office,
Christchurch.

WELLINGTON
The Samaritans,
The Cathedral Office,
Wellington.
Tel: Wellington 49-600

PAKISTAN

KARACHI
Karachi Samaritans,
Selwyn House,
Bonus Road,
Karachi.
Tel: 51420

RHODESIA

BULAWAYO

The Samaritans,
P.O. Box 806,
Bulawayo, Southern Rhodesia
Tel: 5000 (Emergency)
       5001 (Office)

SALISBURY

Salisbury Samaritans,
P.O. Box 981,
Salisbury, Southern Rhodesia.
Tel: 2200

UMTALI

The Samaritans,
12 Cecil Chambers,
Main Street,
Umtali, Southern Rhodesia
Tel: 3559

LIST OF ORGANIZATIONS IN THE UNITED STATES AFFILIATED TO THE 'CENTRE INTERNATIONAL D'INFORMATION DES SERVICES DE SECOURS PAR TELEPHONE'

BOSTON

Rescue, Incorporated,
115 Southampton Street,
Boston 18, Mass.
Tel: HAncock 6.6600

CHICAGO

Suicide Call,
Room 1418,
8 South Michigan,
Chicago, Illin.
Tel: CEntral 6.3044

LOS ANGELES   *Suicide Prevention Center*,
2521 West Pico Boulevard,
Los Angeles 6, Calif.
Tel: DUnkirk 1-5111

MIAMI   *Friends*,
P.O. Box 3606,
Miami, Florida.
Tel: FR 4-3637

NEW YORK   *The Listening Rabbi*,
315 East 72nd Street,
Albany, N.Y.
Tel: TR 9.1124

SALT LAKE CITY   *Salt Lake City Suicide Prevention Center*,
Salt Lake City, Utah.

SAN FRANCISCO   *San Francisco Suicide Prevention
Incorporated*, 965 Geary Street,
San Francisco, Calif.
Tel: PRospect 1.0450

TULSA   *Suicide Prevention Service*,
Box 3501,
Tulsa, Oklah.
Tel: RI 2.2706

WORCESTER   *Rescue, Incorporated*,
(Branch Office),
Worcester, Mass.

LIST OF ORGANIZATIONS ELSEWHERE IN THE WORLD AFFILIATED TO THE 'CENTRE INTERNATIONAL D'INFORMATION DES SERVICES DE SECOURS PAR TELEPHONE'

AUSTRALIA

MELBOURNE
Personal Emergency Supervisory Service,
Alexandra Parade Clinic,
Fitzroy M6—6 Alexandra Parade,
Melbourne.
Tel: 41.5738

SYDNEY
Life Line Centre,
58a Flinders Street,
Darlinghurst,
Sydney.
Tel: 31.0971

BELGIUM

BRUGES
Télé-Accueil,
Télé-Onthaal,
Dyver 8,
Bruges.
Tel: 050.345.00

BRUSSELS
Télé-Accueil,
rue van Maerlant 14,
Brussels.
Tel: 02.35.20.10

MONS
Télé-Accueil,
c/o R. P. Alain,
24 rue Vandervelde,
Cuesmes, près Mons.
Tel: 065.320.20

OSTEND
Télé S.O.S.,
rue de Varsovie 40,
Ostend.
Tel: 059.781.78

BRAZIL

SÃO PAULO   *Campanha de Valorizaçao da Vida,*
rua da Consolaçao 359, C.J.13,
São Paulo.
Tel: 33-5268

DENMARK

AALBORG   *Aalborg Kirketjeneste,*
Budolfi Kirke,
Prestemarken 28,
Aalborg.
Tel: 0011

COPENHAGEN   *Sct. Nicolai Tjenesten,*
Sct. Nicolai Kirke,
Copenhagen.
Tel: Minerva 6393

ODENSE   *Sct. Nicolai Tjenesten,*
Bødtchersrej 25,
Odense.
Tel: 000

FINLAND

HELSINKI   Pastor Jouko Sihvo,
Bockasinvägen 8 A 14,
Drumsö, Helsinki.
Tel: 414135

FRANCE

MARSEILLE   *Amitié S.O.S. par téléphone,*
Boite postale 69,
Marseille-St. Giniez.
Tel: 76.10.10

NICE   *S.O.S. par téléphone,*
Boite postale 19,
Nice.
Tel: 80.28.02

PARIS   *L'Amitié S.O.S. par téléphone,*
               Boite postale 21,
               Boulogne-Billancourt, Seine.
               Tel: 825.70.50

STRASBOURG   *S.O.S. par téléphone,*
               Tel: 34.33.33

GERMANY

BERLIN   *Telefonseelsorge Berlin,*
               IV Obergeschoss, Zimmer 6-7,
               Jebenstr. 1,
               Berlin-Charlottenburg 2.
               Tel: 32.01.55

BREMEN   *Telefonseelsorge Bremen,*
               Hohenloherstr. 9,
               Bremen.
               Tel: 30.30.30

COLOGNE   *Notruf für Verzweifelte,*
               Merlostr. 20,
               Cologne.
               Tel: 73.72.89

DÜSSELDORF   *Telefonseelsorge Düsseldorf,*
               Kaiser-Friedrich-Ring 27,
               Düsseldorf-Oberkassel.
               Tel: 5.15.15

ESSEN   *Ruf und Rat,*
               Schützenbahn 85 III,
               Breckenlinghaus,
               Essen.
               Tel: 24.0.20

FRANKFURT   *Telefon Notruf,*
               Eschenheimer Anlage 21,
               Frankfurt am Main.
               Tel: 55.55.36

HAMBURG   *Telefonseelsorge Hamburg,*
               Katharinenkirchof,
               Hamburg II.
               Tel: 33.73.33

HANOVER

Telefonseelsorge Hannover,
Hubertusstr. 4,
Hanover.
Tel: 66.30.96

KARLSRUHE

Telefonseelsorge Karlsruhe,
Stajerstr. 98,
Karlsruhe.
Tel: 2.33.66

KASSEL

Telefonseelsorge Kassel,
Frankenstr. 18,
Kassel-Wilhelmshöhe.
Tel: 32.40

KIEL

Telefonseelsorge Kiel,
Bartels Allee 7,
Kiel.
Tel: 47.42.22

LUBECK

Telefonseelsorge Lübeck,
Bäckerstr. 3-5,
Lübeck.
Tel: 5.66.44

MANNHEIM

Telefonseelsorge Mannheim,
Traitteurstr. 48,
Mannheim-Ludwigshafen.
Tel: 268.64

Offene Tür,
Breite Strasse,
(Zwischen Marktplatz u. Kaufh. Hansa)
Mannheim F.1, 4.
Tel: 246.90

MUNICH

Telefonseelsorge München,
Kaulbachstr. 31,
Munich 22.
Tel: 29.01.41

NÜRNBERG

Telefonseelsorge Nürnberg,
Pirkheimerstr. 16,
Nürnberg.
Tel: 33.500

STUTTGART
Telefonseelsorge Stuttgart,
Büchsenstr. 36,
Stuttgart N.
Tel: 22.33.33

Ruf und Rat,
Paulinenstr. 40/11,
Stuttgart Süd.

TUBINGEN
Telefonseelsorge Tübingen,
Haus der D.R.K.,
Tübingen.
Tel: 44.44

WIESBADEN
Jugend in Not,
Schutzenhofstr. 9,
Wiesbaden.
Tel: 2.28.46

HOLLAND

ALKMAAR
Telefonische Hulpdienst,
Postbus 87,
Alkmaar.
Tel: (02200) 12502

AMSTERDAM
De Wegwijzer,
Postbus 1209,
Amsterdam.
Tel: (010) 244.444

ARNHEM
Telefonische Hulpdienst,
Velperweg 92,
Arnhem.
Tel: (08.300) 36.000

DELFT
Telefonische Hulpdienst,
Achterom 78,
Delft.
Tel: (01730) 31.222

DORDRECHT
Telefonische Hulpdienst,
Adr. van Bleijenburghstraat 24,
Dordrecht.
Tel: (01850) 2.11.22

GRONINGEN *S.O.S. Telefon,*
Helper brink 15,
Groningen.
Tel: (05900) 450.000

HAARLEM *Telefonische Hulpdienst,*
Kendupark 24,
Haarlem.
Tel: (02500) 22.0.22

THE HAGUE *S.O.S. Telefon,*
Van der Duynstraat 177,
The Hague.
Tel: (070) 18.22.66

HILVERSUM *I.K.O.R.,*
Oranjelaan 8,
Hilversum.
Tel: (02950) 1.55.55

NIJMEGEN *Telefonische Hulpdienst,*
Regentessestraat 27,
Nijmegen.
Tel: (08800) 28280

ROTTERDAM *Telefonische Hulpdienst,*
Westersingel 109,
Rotterdam.
Tel: (010) 12.14.14

UTRECHT *Telefonische Hulpdienst S.O.S.,*
Weerdsingel—O.Z. 34,
Utrecht.
Tel: (030) 123.00

ZAANSTREEK *Telefonische Hulpdienst,*
Beukenweg,
Zaanstreek.
Tel: (02980) 62.000

ITALY

FLORENCE *Telefono Amico,*
Florence.
Tel: 48.34.30

GENOA
Telefono Amico,
Genoa.
Tel: 59.58.58

MILAN
Telefono Amico,
Milan.
Tel: 688.2155

MEXICO

MEXICO CITY
A.M.A.D.,
LIverpool 25,
Mexico—6 D.F.
Tel: 46.40.46

NORWAY

OSLO
Kirkens Nottjeneste,
Oslo Indremisjon,
Maridalsveien 33,
Oslo.
Tel: 33.13.80

SOUTH AFRICA

JOHANNESBURG
Suicides Anonymous (TVL),
201 Castle Mansion—Eloff Street,
Johannesburg.
Tel: 22.288

SWEDEN

BORAS
Jourhavande Präst,
Nelsonssgatan 3,
Boras.
Tel: 90000 (Emergency)
       033-16310 (Office)

GAVLE
Jourhavande Präst,
Gavle.
Tel: 90000 (Emergency)

243

GOTHENBERG   *Jourhavande Präst,*
Cederbourgsgatan 8,
Gothenberg.
Tel: 90000 (Emergency)
031-169080 (Office)

MALMÖ   *Ankaret Radgivning,*
Föreningsgatan 71,
Malmö.
Tel: 35.050 (Emergency)
040-14332 (Office)

NORRKÖPING   *Jourhavande Präst,*
Winkelsgatan 22,
Norrköping.
Tel: 90000 (Emergency)
011-37973 (Office)

OREBRO   *Prästernas Jourtjänst,*
Längbro, Brastgard,
Orebro.
Tel: 90000 (Emergency)
019-42000 (Office)

SANDVIKEN   *Jourhavande Präst,*
Asgatan 11,
Sandviken.
Tel: 90000 (Emergency)
026-54453 (Office)

SODERTALJE   *Jourhavande Präst,*
Bellevuegatan 2,
Sodertalje.
Tel: 90000 (Emergency)
0755-38063 (Office)

STOCKHOLM   *Jourhavande Präst,*
Sturevägen 48, Enebyberg,
Stockholm.
Tel: 90000 (Emergency)
113033 (Office)

Kristen Radgivning,
Tognérgatan 34,
Stockholm VA.
Tel: 340294

TOARPSDAL   *The Suicide Pastor,*
             Eksbo,
             Toarpsdal.

TRELLEBORG   *Kyrkoherde Egan Eberhard,*
             Gamla Torg 2,
             Trelleborg.
             Tel: 17000 (Emergency)
                  0410-13904 (Office)

UPPSALA   *Jourhavande Präst,*
             Samariterhemmet,
             Uppsala.
             Tel: 90000 (Emergency)

SWITZERLAND

AARAU   *Die Dargebotene Hand,*
             Hallwylstr. 11,
             Aarau.
             Tel: 064. 22. 88. 88

BERNE   *Die Dargebotene Hand,*
             Turnweg 14,
             Berne.
             Tel: 031.23.12.23

BIENNE/BIEL *Die Dargebotene Hand,*
             La Main Tendue,
             Sägefeldweg 14,
             Boite postale 500,
             Bienne/Biel.
             Tel: 032.3.55.55

LA CHAUX-DE- *La Main Tendue,*
FONDS   Case postale Charrière,
              La Chaux-de-Fonds.
              Tel: 039.3.11.44

GENEVA   *La Main Tendue,*
             Case postale 62,
             Geneva.
             Tel: 022.33.81.33

LAUSANNE

Fraternité St. Martin,
2 rue St. Laurent,
Lausanne.

LUCERNE

Die Dargebotene Hand,
Hirschmattstr. 1,
Lucerne.
Tel: 041.3.76.75

ST. GALLEN

Die Dargebotene Hand,
Melonenstr. 9,
St. Gallen.
Tel: 071.23.14.14

SEEWIS

Die Dargebotene Hand,
Seewis im Prätigau.
Tel: 081.5.23.77

WINTERTHUR

Die Dargebotene Hand,
Hufteggstr. 19,
Winterthur.
Tel: 052.9.11.11

ZURICH

Die Dargebotene Hand,
Hotzestr. 56,
Zurich.
Tel: 051.26.20.00

TURKEY

ISTANBUL

Canyoldaslar Cemiyeti,
Operatör Raif Bey Sok 45/7,
Sisli,
Istanbul.
Tel: 47.68.58
(This is a Branch
of The Samaritans)

ALSO PUBLISHED BY CONSTABLE

The true wilderness

By H. A. Williams

"This book will, I believe, establish itself as one of the spiritual classics of the twentieth century. It seems to me that anyone who reads it with serious attention cannot put the volume down without a measure of beneficial (if more or less painful) self-awareness, and without a real enlargement of his vision of life.

"The central importance of this book is that here is an original proclamation of the Christian faith that is radical and yet consonant with the core of traditional Christianity. Here is positive affirmation instead of the arid agnosticism that underlies much 'modern' theology. Above all, this book rings true with notes of personal integrity and exact description that are as rare as they are inspiring."
Hugh Montefiore, Cambridge Review

"He writes simply, clearly and startlingly, so that each of his sermons is like an exciting and amusing short story, holding one to the last sentence."
John Betjeman, The Spectator   (3rd impression)

Beyond all reason

A personal experience of madness

By Morag Coate

"A book of rare insight and almost incredible courage . . . a uniquely important human documentary—comforting, alarming, stimulating and immensely readable. I hope all intelligent lovers of humanity will read it."
J. B. Phillips

The faith of the counsellors

By Paul Halmos

A study of the beliefs, theories, and influence on the community of social caseworkers, psychotherapists, psychiatrists, probation officers, marriage guidance counsellors, and all those who help others professionally with their problems.

Honesty in the Church

By Daniel Callahan

A Catholic layman's discourse on the dilemmas and tensions of Christian freedom.

"A most sensitive book, whose passionate and compassionate concern for integrity is summed up in his description of the responsibility of the Church: 'to make honesty possible so that no Catholic is forced to leave the Church before the Church has suffered with him'."
The Bishop of Woolwich

Objections to Christian belief

Edited with an Introduction by A. R. Vidler

Contributors: D. M. MacKinnon, H. A. Williams, J. S. Bezzant

"A book that leaves the effect of a moral and intellectual spring-clean . . . the work of Christians deliberately exposing themselves, because they love what they trust and trust what they love.'
The Bishop of Woolwich

"Likely to remain a source book of the New Theology."
Twentieth Century   (6th impression)

Objections to Humanism

Edited with an Introduction by H. J. Blackham

Contributors: Ronald Hepburn, Kingsley Martin, Kathleen Nott

"One may salute the austerely brave spirit behind such a book as this, and then keep it as a very handy statement of what Humanism at its best believes about life and about men."
The Church Times   (2nd impression)

Objections to Roman Catholicism

Edited with an Introduction by Michael de la Bedoyere

Contributors: Magdalen Goffin, John Todd, H. P. R. Finberg, Frank Roberts, Rosemary Haughton, G. F. Pollard, Archbishop Thomas Roberts, SJ. "Likely to have the same impact on Catholics as *Honest to God* had on Anglicans." *Geoffrey Moorhouse, The Guardian* (4th impression)